"I used to think sliders were only mini hamburgers that were passed around at parties, but Jon Melendez has proved to the world that they can be so much more. He has given me the tools to eat more and more of my favorite mini food."

—Adrianna Adarme, author of *The Year of Cozy: 125 Recipes, Crafts, and Other Homemade Adventures*

the
SLIDER
EFFECT

to mamma, jen, and nick:
THE THREE MOST IMPORTANT WOMEN
IN MY LIFE. I WOULDN'T KNOW LOVE
IF IT WEREN'T FOR YOU.

the
SLIDER
EFFECT

| you can't eat just one |

JONATHAN MELENDEZ

PHOTOGRAPHY BY JONATHAN MELENDEZ

Andrews McMeel
Publishing®

a division of Andrews McMeel Universal

contents

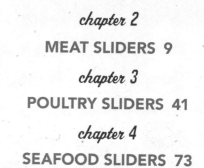

how to use this book to make the best sliders and be the rock star you know you are!

| a.k.a. the basics |

introduction

If you're holding this book in your hands, chances are you bought it or someone gave it to you as a gift. (In which case you should probably keep that someone in your life forever, or at the very least, name your next child after him or her; he/she happens to have great taste in books.) If you're holding this book while standing in the middle of a store, and contemplating whether you should purchase it or not, the answer is yes, you should definitely buy it. Treat yourself; it'll be the best decision you've ever made. The second-best decision you'll make will be to cook your way through the entire book. If you're holding this book in your hands and you're thinking to yourself, "Why sliders?," we'll get to that in a second. The real question you should be asking yourself is, "How can I become a slider pro?!" Before I go on to answer both those questions, let me tell you more about this book.

The Slider Effect is a form of thinking and a way of life. It's how sliders are different than burgers, because I think it's really important to mention that sliders aren't just mini burgers. The Slider Effect proves that sliders are the perfect bite, and when made correctly, they allow people to evenly taste all the layers of flavor they have in between two buns. There is no right or wrong way to go through and cook from this book. As you'll quickly come to realize, the ultimate goal is to have fun because sliders are meant to be enjoyable. My passion for sliders has grown so immense that if a slider is on a menu, I'm ordering it without question. I love everything that sliders represent. They have the power to bring people together and get them really excited about eating. The fact that I finally get to share my passion with you—yes, you holding this book and reading these words—is a dream come true.

WHY SLIDERS?

Sliders have become so popular in recent culture thanks to a rise in gastro pubs, tapas restaurants, and bars that focus on shared plates and craft cocktails. It's a lot more fun when you can order a couple of drinks, pick a variety of appetizers, and share them around the table with friends. Sliders are the ultimate food experience because they work as an appetizer, as a snack, or for breakfast, lunch, or dinner. They're great any time of day, whether you're just a tad bit hungry and in need of a small bite, or starving and want to devour about ten of them in one sitting. Sliders are the perfect party food because you can easily offer your guests a variety of flavors and different options that suit anyone's dietary restrictions. They're easily adaptable and are a definite crowd pleaser. They're no longer merely a predinner food that you order at a restaurant with just beef and cheese—they've now become hip, cool, and even somewhat upscale. Perfect for any occasion, sliders are the answer to your everyday life.

I didn't want to give you a book just on sliders, though, and call it a day. Instead, this book is an all-encompassing cookbook on one of my all-time

favorite foods, and everything that comes with it. *The Slider Effect* focuses on more than just ordinary cheeseburger sliders, the ones we're all used to seeing on menus and eating. The recipes in this book will change the way we as a culture look at sliders. With four chapters on sliders—Meat, Poultry, Seafood, and Vegetarian—the book transforms classic everyday dishes such as eggplant Parmesan, fish and chips, chicken-fried steak, and curry into tiny versions sandwiched between homemade buns and layered with various easy-to-make sauces and spreads. I want you to feel confident enough to get in that kitchen of yours and tackle any one—and hopefully all—of these recipes. The goal here is to take the fear out of baking homemade bread and making sauces from scratch and instead to make you feel like you can conquer anything in the kitchen. Through these pages, you'll find everything you need to know on how to become a slider pro. When you're done, you'll not only impress your family and friends, you'll also impress yourself, and your stomach.

HOW TO USE THIS BOOK

There are two ways to use this book. First, make the sliders the way I've mapped them out for you. Follow the recipes as they're written and enjoy some of the best sliders you'll ever have. Each slider is listed with a suggested bun and sauce. Get comfortable with the recipes, and get to know them before you start mixing them up.

Then, forget about everything you've learned. You're the boss now and you have the power to decide what goes in and on your sliders. If you don't like the bun I used for a certain recipe, then ditch it. Make and use another bun, roll, or biscuit from Chapter 6, or grab something from the grocery store. Cooking is much more fun when you're adventurous and can give each recipe your personal touch. The same thing goes for the sauces, spreads, and condiments in Chapter 7. Switch them up among the various sliders to create new and unique slider combinations customized to fit your taste buds. I intentionally created the components—like the buns and sauces—in this book to be interchangeable. I want the book to be interactive and above all, fun for you.

With that said, I think it's important to talk about what you need in order to get the most out of this cookbook. I'm always being asked what I have in my pantry or what kitchen equipment and tools I use on a regular basis. "Jonathan, what are your go-to spices and herbs? Jonathan, what kitchen equipment do you use the most?" Okay, so it's mostly my mom who asks, but that still counts, so it's definitely worth mentioning. In the book I specify a few pantry items and kitchen equipment several times, so I thought it would be a great idea to list them all here, before you dive into the recipes. That way you'll be prepared and won't feel like you're caught off guard.

pantry essentials

SEASONINGS

This is a great place to start, since flavor is most important when it comes to sliders. A friend once told me that she tends to underseason everything she makes because she is afraid of doing it wrong, or worse, overdoing it. Seasoning your food doesn't have to be scary. In fact, nothing is scarier than bland, underseasoned food. Remember that. Here are a few seasonings that I can't cook without.

SALT

I find there are two extremes when it comes to home cooks using salt. We either don't use enough, so everything tastes sort of bland and the same, or we use way too much. The best piece of advice I can give you is to salt as you go and to season every step of the way. Okay, so that's two pieces of advice. Sure, salt can be frightening, and it does get a bad rap of being "bad for us," but there's nothing to be afraid of. A well-seasoned meal can be magical. So what kind of salt do I use? When I'm cooking, I always reach for kosher salt. I like the coarseness of it, and I feel like I need less because of the bigger texture. For baking, I turn to good ole iodized table salt. The grains are fine, allowing the salt to be distributed evenly among the dry ingredients.

BLACK PEPPER

I'm black pepper's biggest fan. I will literally put it on everything, but let's get one thing straight: That powdered black pepper sold in those little spice canisters at the grocery store does not have the same flavor or texture as fresh, coarsely ground black pepper. So if you have the powdered kind in your cupboard right now, go over and toss it in the trash. You'll be doing yourself a favor. Bottom line: Always grind your black pepper fresh from whole peppercorns. You'll be surprised by the difference in flavor.

GRANULATED GARLIC AND GRANULATED ONION

You'll notice that throughout the book I use a lot of granulated garlic and granulated onion and sometimes even garlic powder and onion powder. The powder variety is basically the same thing as granulated, only it's more finely ground. When I want the seasoning to be fully incorporated into the dish, I use powder, but when I want a bit of texture, I'll use granulated. They're my go-to seasonings (aside from salt and pepper). Maybe it's because they provide so much flavor to anything, without any effort at all. You can take your food from meh to whoa, in an instant. I think everyone should keep them both in their pantry. One very important note to consider: Don't confuse the granulated or powdered versions with garlic salt and onion salt. Those are completely different. I tend to stay away from seasonings that have the word "salt" in them because whenever I use them, I can't control the amount of salt going into my food. I don't know exactly how much salt is in those packaged spice containers. Then questions arise like, "Is there enough salt in this dish? Should I add more? Is there too much salt now?" We shouldn't feel stumped in our own kitchen.

FRESH HERBS VS. DRY HERBS

Whenever possible, use fresh herbs. They're always 100 times better than their dried counterparts. That's not to say that I'm totally against dried herbs. I think there is a time and a place for them. If I'm making a dry rub for meat or fish and want all the seasoning and herbs to blend together easily, I'll go for the dry. If I want to add a pop of freshness and color to a stew or soup, I'll reach for the fresh herbs. A rule of thumb to keep in mind is that dried herbs are generally more potent and concentrated, so you'll use less than you would fresh herbs.

PARSLEY

Parsley gets its own special mention because I use it a lot, and not just for garnish or finishing touches. It adds great flavor to sauces, stews, or soups. When it comes to deciding which to use, I always go with flat-leaf Italian parsley. It has more flavor than the curly variety. Plus I think it looks a bit better when chopped and stirred into dishes or sauces.

OILS

I always keep a few different kinds of oil in my pantry, each with a specific use and purpose. I use olive oil for sautéing and most low to moderate heat cooking. I grab the extra-virgin olive oil for dressing salads or making condiments and sauces. Lastly, vegetable or canola oil for deep-frying or high heat cooking because it won't burn like low-smoke-point oils or affect the taste of certain dishes.

equipment

BAKING SHEETS

Invest in sturdy, high-quality baking sheets. This will change the way you bake. Some of those cheap, flimsy cookie sheets aren't good because they bake things unevenly and tend to warp and bend in the oven. They're so thin that the heat goes directly through the pan, causing the bottom of the cookies to burn. High-quality baking sheets don't mean

you have to empty your bank account. You can find professional-quality baking sheets online or at your local restaurant supply store for a lot less. I recommend grabbing a few half-sheet baking pans and quarter-sheet baking pans. I use both of them almost daily for a lot more than just baking. They're also great as a place to set gathered ingredients or to rest cooked food. They can be quite versatile.

WIRE COOLING RACKS

Wire cooling racks do so much more than cool cookies right out of the oven. I place them on top of baking sheets and use them to air-dry dredged pieces of meat or vegetables, so that the coating adheres. They also keep fried foods from getting soggy, a crucial component of many of the sliders in the book.

STOVETOP GRILL PAN

If you don't have an outdoor grill or just don't have space for an outdoor grill because you live in an apartment without a balcony, then your new best friend is a grill pan for the stovetop. I like using one made of cast iron because it's sturdy and heavy-duty. Simply treat it like you would a regular cast-iron skillet and don't leave it soaking because it'll rust on you. Make sure to clean it with warm water (without dish soap because it'll strip the seasoning off) after each use. You'll be able to get those golden brown grill marks without a big bulky outdoor grill during any season. Just make sure to turn on the vent and have a towel handy in case the smoke detectors go off. It has happened to me more times than I'd care to admit.

DEEP-FRY THERMOMETER

There is quite a bit of frying in this book. Before you start getting scared, though, grab yourself a candy/deep-fry thermometer because it'll take away a lot of that fear. Many people fry in oil that is the wrong temperature, and that's when they run into all sorts of problems—like the outside getting too brown before the inside is fully cooked. If you moderate the temperature of your oil, you'll have a much smoother frying experience.

PEPPER MILL

The most precious kitchen gadget you can purchase is a pepper mill. That little gadget alone is worth more than any of those super-expensive stainless steel pots and pans you have your eye on. Believe me. Pick one up that coarsely grinds the peppercorns so that you can have a bit more texture to your freshly ground black pepper.

FOIL, PLASTIC WRAP, AND PARCHMENT PAPER

As conveniences, these are very important to have on hand in order to be a successful at-home cook. I wouldn't be able to cook without any of them. Aluminum foil is important if only because it saves you from cleaning baking sheets (a lazy cook's dream); it also helps keep certain foods warm. Plastic wrap is crucial for creating an airtight seal on dishes or sauces that need to be covered and stored. It helps keep things fresh longer. Parchment paper saves you lots of heartache and suffering when removing baked goods from baking sheets.

Now that you know the basics and are well equipped, it's time to go out and conquer the world, one slider at a time. The most important thing to remember is that you need to have fun. The kitchen doesn't have to be a daunting place. If for some reason you mess up, it's all good. Stop, laugh about it, and start over. Make sure to read through each of the recipes carefully before you begin—that way you familiarize yourself with the steps and ingredients beforehand. Once you're comfortable, put on that apron (yes, anyone can look good in an apron), grab your utensils, and set forth.

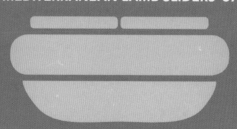

meat sliders

I don't want to throw around the word "favorite" too much because then it starts to lose its luster. So I'll be very selective about saying what is indeed my favorite anything. But right here, right out of the gate, without wasting any time: This is my favorite chapter. I'm a carnivore at heart, and although the other chapters are near and dear to me, this one right here is my first true love. So it's no surprise that the meat chapter comes first in the book.

This chapter is made up of beef, pork, and lamb sliders that combine traditional and unique flavors in a tiny bite—far from the classic cheeseburger sliders we're all used to eating. For instance, the Grilled Steak and Potato Sliders (page 22) layer slices of grilled flank steak, grilled potatoes, crisp lettuce, crumbled blue cheese, and Chimichurri (page 168). It's a steak house in slider form. American Breakfast Sliders (page 10), made with eggs, bacon or sausage, and cheese, are a prime example that sliders can also be a breakfast food. There's no wrong or right way when it comes to eating sliders. You'll quickly learn that there's no shortage of flavor in this chapter.

american breakfast sliders

YIELD: **12 sliders**

12 large eggs

¼ cup whole milk or half-and-half

1 teaspoon kosher salt

1 teaspoon coarsely ground black pepper

Couple dashes of hot sauce

4 tablespoons unsalted butter

12 Whole Wheat English Muffins (page 142) or store-bought biscuits or rolls

Roasted Garlic Aioli (page 162), or ¼ cup mayonnaise

Sweet and Spicy Strawberry-Rhubarb Tomato Ketchup (page 171), or ¼ cup ketchup (optional)

6 (4 by 4-inch) slices cheddar cheese, cut in half crosswise

6 slices bacon, cut in half and cooked until crispy, or 12 cooked breakfast sausage patties

I've been cooking and experimenting with food for over ten years now. However, no matter how many fancy dishes I learn how to make, for some unknown reason, a simple English muffin breakfast sandwich is one of the things I crave the most first thing in the morning. I would beg my mama for a fast-food breakfast sandwich each week on my way to school. On very few occasions she'd give in, and I'd be the happiest kid alive. Now, as an adult, I'm making them at home, in slider form, with mini Whole Wheat English Muffins (page 142), which makes me feel better about my morning choices.

1. In a large mixing bowl, whisk together the eggs, milk, salt, pepper, and hot sauce until fully combined.

2. Set a large skillet over medium-high heat and add the butter. Once melted, add the eggs and stir with a heatproof spatula. Decrease the heat to low and cook untouched for about 4 minutes. Once the eggs start to set around the edges, bring the sides in toward the center. Continue to cook for 8 to 10 minutes, or until no longer runny.

3. Preheat the oven to 325°F. Grease a 9 by 13-inch baking sheet and set aside.

4. Pour the whisked egg mixture into a prepared baking dish and bake for 40 to 45 minutes, or until a knife inserted in the middle comes out clean. Let cool slightly and then cut into 2-inch rounds using a round biscuit or cookie cutter.

try these sliders with:

Everything Bagel Slider
Buns (page 138)

Black Pepper Buttermilk
Biscuits (page 145)

Waffle Buns (page 144)

Chimichurri (page 168)

5. To assemble the sliders, split the English muffins and toast. Spread both halves of the muffins with aioli, and ketchup, if using. Divide the scrambled eggs evenly among the bottom halves of the muffins. Top each with 2 pieces of cheese, and 2 half-slices of bacon or a sausage patty. Replace the top halves of the English muffins, and skewer with a long toothpick. Serve immediately.

chicken-fried steak sliders

YIELD: **12 sliders**

STEAK

4 (4-ounce) cube steaks

1½ teaspoons kosher salt, divided

1½ teaspoons coarsely ground black pepper, divided

1 cup all-purpose flour

¼ cup cornstarch

½ teaspoon cayenne pepper

2 large eggs

2 tablespoons whole milk

Couple dashes of hot sauce

Vegetable oil, for frying

GRAVY

4 pork breakfast sausage links

1 small yellow onion, minced

2 tablespoons all-purpose flour

1 cup whole milk

½ teaspoon kosher salt

½ teaspoon coarsely ground black pepper

12 Black Pepper Buttermilk Biscuits (page 145) or store-bought biscuits

Roasted Garlic Aioli (page 162)

Seeing chicken-fried steak on a menu as a kid always confused me. Several thoughts went through my mind: Is it chicken? Is it steak? Do I want to eat it? Will I like it? I would end up ordering it either way because I was curious, but even after I ate it, I still wasn't sure what it was. One thing I was sure about, though, was that I loved it. It tasted just like fried chicken to me, which I think is the point. Now, as an adult, I know it's beef, and my love for it has not wavered. The only difference is that I'm sticking it between halves of a biscuit, loading it with garlic aioli and sausage gravy, and calling it a slider.

1. To prepare the steak, cut the cube steaks into 2-inch squares. Arrange on a baking sheet and season lightly on both sides with 1 teaspoon of the salt and 1 teaspoon of the black pepper.

2. Combine the flour, cornstarch, cayenne, and the remaining ¼ teaspoon salt and ¼ teaspoon black pepper. In a separate dish, whisk the eggs, milk, hot sauce, ¼ teaspoon salt, and ¼ teaspoon black pepper in a shallow bowl or dish.

3. Prepare 2 baking pans by placing a wire rack in each; set aside. Dredge the steak by dipping the pieces first into the flour mixture, then into the egg, and once again into the flour. Shake to remove excess flour and arrange on a wire rack. Continue dredging the steak until all the pieces are coated. Let sit for about 10 minutes.

continued on page 14

chicken-fried steak sliders
continued

4. Preheat the oven to 250°F. Fill a large cast-iron skillet with enough oil to fill just about halfway up, and place over medium-high heat. Once the oil is hot, carefully lay in a few pieces of the breaded steak at a time. Fry for 2 to 4 minutes, or until golden brown, flip, and fry for another 2 to 3 minutes on the second side. Drain and transfer to the second prepared pan. Continue in this manner until all of the pieces are fried. Keep the steak warm in the oven while you prepare the gravy.

5. To make the gravy, cook the sausage in a saucepan over medium-high heat until brown and crispy, 8 to 10 minutes. Add the onion and cook for another minute or two. Stir in the flour until well combined. Slowly stream in the milk, while stirring, until well combined. Simmer over low heat until the gravy thickens. Season with salt and pepper.

6. To assemble the sliders, split the biscuits in half and liberally spread with aioli. Top with a piece or two of the chicken-fried steak and spoon the gravy over each. Cover with the top of the biscuits and serve immediately.

TIP: The cornstarch in the flour coating makes this chicken-fried steak extra crunchy. Try adding cornstarch to your flour mixture the next time you're coating and frying chicken, pork chops, or shrimp.

NOTE: The Black Pepper Buttermilk Biscuits (page 145) yield 9 biscuits, so you'll need to make a double batch for this recipe.

try these sliders with:

Baked-Potato Buttermilk
Biscuits (page 156)

Pretzel Buns (page 146)

Classic Potato Rolls (page 154)

Sweet and Spicy Honey
Mustard (page 170)

bbq pulled-pork sliders

YIELD: **12 sliders**

PULLED PORK

1 tablespoon kosher salt

1 teaspoon coarsely
ground black pepper

1 teaspoon granulated garlic

1 teaspoon granulated onion

¼ teaspoon cayenne pepper

1 teaspoon mustard powder

½ teaspoon ground cumin

1 (3 to 3½-pound) boneless
pork shoulder

2 tablespoons vegetable or canola oil

1 large yellow onion, diced

4 garlic cloves, smashed and peeled

¼ cup tomato paste

½ cup apple cider vinegar

2 cups chicken broth or stock

One of my guilty pleasures is going to a barbecue joint and ordering pulled pork, ribs, a sausage link, and one of each of the sides and eating it all by myself. The best part is that I get to eat with my hands and feel like a caveman. Sure, there might be barbecue sauce all over my face, but it's worth it. If you ever wondered what the ultimate food truck slider would be, it's this one. Pulled pork smothered in barbecue sauce, topped with slaw and pickles, all held together by crispy waffles. Yes, waffles.

---

1. To make the pulled pork, in a small bowl, combine the salt, black pepper, granulated garlic, granulated onion, cayenne pepper, mustard powder, and cumin. Rub the pork shoulder with the seasoning mixture and let sit at room temperature for 1 hour.

2. Preheat the oven to 300°F. Set a 6-quart Dutch oven over medium-high heat and pour in the oil. Once hot, carefully place the pork shoulder in, and brown on each side, 5 to 6 minutes total. Transfer to a plate and set aside. Add the onion, garlic, and tomato paste to the pot and cook, stirring constantly, for 1 minute. Stir in the vinegar and chicken broth and bring to a simmer. Remove from the heat, return the pork to the pot, cover, and transfer to the oven. Cook until tender and the meat starts to fall apart, about 3 hours total, turning the pork over every hour.

continued on page 16

bbq pulled-pork sliders

continued

CREAMY BROCCOLI SLAW

1 (6-ounce) bag broccoli slaw mix

½ small red cabbage, finely shredded

½ cup plain Greek yogurt

¼ cup mayonnaise

1 tablespoon sugar

1 tablespoon fresh lemon juice

½ teaspoon salt

½ teaspoon coarsely
ground black pepper

SLIDERS

12 Waffle Buns (page 144, see Note),
or 6 frozen Belgian waffles cut into
quarters or store-bought dinner rolls

Barbecue Sauce (page 164), or
1 cup store-bought barbecue sauce

---

try these sliders with:

Braided Challah Buns (page 140)

Pretzel Buns (page 146)

Sweet Pineapple Hawaiian
Rolls (page 152)

Sweet and Spicy Strawberry-Rhubarb
Tomato Ketchup (page 171)

---

3. Meanwhile, make the broccoli slaw. In a large bowl, stir together the broccoli slaw mix, cabbage, yogurt, mayonnaise, sugar, lemon juice, salt, and pepper until combined. Cover and let chill until ready to use. This can be made a day or two in advance.

4. Once the pork is done, carefully transfer it to a cutting board. Shred with 2 forks and return to the pot.

5. To assemble the sliders, spread all of the waffles with barbecue sauce. Add a mound of the pulled pork to half of the waffles and top with a spoonful of slaw. Place another waffle on top of each and skewer with a long toothpick to hold in place. Serve immediately.

NOTE: For this recipe, make the Waffle Buns as directed but omit the scallions, bacon, and cheddar. These sliders are best with plain waffles!

lasagna sliders

1½ pounds hot Italian ground sausage

1 cup ricotta cheese

1 teaspoon finely grated lemon zest

1 tablespoon fresh lemon juice

2 tablespoons chopped fresh basil

1 garlic clove, minced

½ teaspoon kosher salt

¼ teaspoon coarsely
ground black pepper

Red Wine Marinara (page 169)

12 Rosemary Parmesan Focaccia
Buns (page 148) or store-
bought ciabatta rolls

1 cup shredded mozzarella

One of my New Year's resolutions each year is to make lasagna. It never happens, though, which is why that resolution makes an appearance on the top of my list year after year. Why is it that lasagna always ends up taking an entire day to make? No one has that kind of time. That's why I've taken all of my favorite lasagna flavors—marinara, spicy Italian sausage, ricotta, and basil—and turned them into a fun slider. Lasagna just got easier to make.

---

1. Divide the ground sausage into 12 even portions. Working with one portion at a time, roll the sausage into a ball and then shape into a 2-inch-wide patty with the palms of your hands. Place on a baking sheet and continue forming the rest.

2. Place a large skillet over medium-high heat. Once hot, cook the sausage patties, a few at a time, for 4 to 5 minutes, or until crispy and dark brown. Flip over and cook for another 2 to 3 minutes on the second side. Continue cooking the rest in the same manner.

3. In a medium bowl, combine the ricotta, lemon zest, lemon juice, basil, garlic, salt, and pepper.

4. Place the marinara in a small saucepan over low heat and cook until warmed through, about 5 minutes.

try these sliders with:

Braided Challah Buns (page 140)

Pretzel Buns (page 146)

Crusty French Bread Rolls (page 150)

Arugula Pumpkin Seed
Pesto (page 167)

5. To assemble the sliders, split the buns and spread about a tablespoon of the ricotta mixture onto the bottom half of the buns. Top with a sausage patty, mozzarella, warmed marinara sauce, and the top half of the bun. Skewer with a long toothpick to hold it all in place. Serve immediately or at room temperature.

hot dog sliders

YIELD: **12 sliders**

6 large hot dogs or cooked bratwursts

2 tablespoons olive oil

12 Pretzel Buns (page 146) or store-bought dinner rolls, warmed

Sweet and Spicy Honey Mustard (page 170)

1 (15-ounce) jar sauerkraut, drained

1 (16-ounce) jar dill pickle chips, drained

1 small yellow onion, diced

try these sliders with:

Everything Bagel Slider Buns (page 138)

Sweet Pineapple Hawaiian Rolls (page 152)

Classic Potato Rolls (page 154)

Sweet and Spicy Strawberry-Rhubarb Tomato Ketchup (page 171)

It doesn't get any more American than hot dogs and hamburgers. Stick an American flag in my hat and call me "macaroni." That's why I decided to combine the two into a slider—because it just felt like the right thing to do. Use this recipe as a base but change it up as you see fit. I know that we can all be very particular when it comes to our hot dog toppings of choice, so feel free to use whatever you like.

1. Cut each hot dog or bratwurst in half and then butterfly-cut each half (cutting lengthwise but not all the way through, just enough to flatten the hot dog).

2. Set a grill pan, griddle, or skillet over medium-high heat and add the olive oil. Once hot, place the hot dogs in the pan, flat side down. Cook in batches until crispy and browned on both sides, 4 to 5 minutes per batch.

3. To assemble the sliders, split the buns in half and spread each half with mustard. Place a hot dog piece on the bottom half of each bun. Top with sauerkraut, a few pickle chips, and a spoonful of onion. Sandwich together with the top bun and secure with a long toothpick to hold in place. Serve immediately.

grilled steak and potato sliders

YIELD: 12 sliders

3 pounds flank steak

3 tablespoons olive oil, divided

3 or 4 medium Yukon gold potatoes, scrubbed

2 teaspoons kosher salt

1½ teaspoons coarsely ground black pepper

12 Crusty French Bread Rolls (page 150) or store-bought French bread rolls

Cilantro, Lime, and Green Chili Aioli (page 162)

Chimichurri (page 168)

½ cup crumbled blue cheese

6 romaine lettuce leaves, cut in half

Sometimes I wish I'd been born somewhere in the Midwest, just so I would have a valid excuse to eat meat and potatoes all day long. Don't get me wrong: I still eat meat and potatoes on a regular basis even though I was born in California and not in the Midwest. Potatoes count as a vegetable, right? If you can't find flank steak at the grocery store, try this with skirt steak or a T-bone. It's also great with grilled chicken or pork if you're not a big fan of red meat.

1. Pat the flank steak dry with a few paper towels. Drizzle and rub both sides of the steak with 2 tablespoons of the olive oil. Season both sides well with salt and pepper. Place in a large resealable plastic bag and chill in the refrigerator for at least 4 hours, or overnight.

2. Place the potatoes in a large saucepan and cover with cold water. Set over medium-high heat and bring to a boil. Lower the heat and simmer until a little under fork-tender. Drain and let cool down completely. Cut into ½-inch-thick slices and drizzle with the remaining tablespoon of olive oil; set aside.

3. Remove the steak from the refrigerator and let stand at room temperature for at least 45 minutes before grilling. Heat an outdoor grill or stovetop grill pan over medium-high heat. Grill the steak (without moving or touching it) for 4 to 5 minutes. Flip over and continue to cook for another 4 to 6 minutes on the second side for medium. Remove from the heat, cover loosely with aluminum foil, and let rest for about 5 minutes before slicing. Slice the steak, against the grain, into thin slices.

4. Meanwhile, grill the potatoes on each side just until grill marks form, 2 to 3 minutes total.

5. To assemble the sliders, split the rolls in half and spread each half generously with the aioli and chimichurri. Place a grilled potato slice on the bottom half of each roll, a few slices of steak, and top with blue cheese, lettuce, and the top half of each roll. Skewer together with a long toothpick to hold in place. Serve immediately or at room temperature.

vietnamese banh mi sliders

YIELD: 12 sliders

PICKLED VEGETABLES

2 large carrots, peeled and julienned

1 medium daikon radish, peeled and julienned

4 tablespoons plus 3 teaspoons sugar, divided

1 teaspoon kosher salt

½ cup white rice vinegar

½ cup warm water

I'm a soup-and-sandwich kind of guy. Whenever I have a bowl of soup, I need to have a small sandwich to pair with it for dipping and dunking. On *pho* nights, I'll always order a bowl of *pho* and a *banh mi* sandwich, which are these incredibly delicious Vietnamese sandwiches that are traditionally made with Vietnamese cold cuts like sliced pork, pork belly, and liver pâté and fresh veggies like carrots, cucumber, daikon, and cilantro. These sliders are made with ground pork and flavored with the same ingredients in a traditional *banh mi*. All that is missing is the *pho*.

SLIDERS

2 pounds ground pork

3 tablespoons chili garlic sauce

1 tablespoon Asian fish sauce

1 tablespoon fresh lime juice

2 teaspoons sugar

3 tablespoons canola or vegetable oil, for brushing

12 Crusty French Bread Rolls (page 150) or store-bought crusty rolls

Sriracha Aioli (page 162), or ½ cup mayonnaise

½ medium English cucumber, thinly sliced

2 medium jalapeños, thinly sliced

¾ cup loosely packed cilantro leaves

12 thin slices Black Forest ham

––––––––––––––

try these sliders with:

Braided Challah Buns (page 140)

Waffle Buns (page 144)

Classic Potato Rolls (page 154)

Sweet and Spicy Honey Mustard (page 170)

––––––––––––––

1. To make the pickled vegetables, in a large bowl, toss together the carrots, daikon, 3 teaspoons of the sugar, and the salt. Let sit for 5 minutes to release their natural water, soften, and lose some of their volume. Drain in a colander and press down a bit to release any excess liquid. Return to the bowl and combine with the remaining 4 tablespoons of sugar, the vinegar, and water. The vegetables should be completely covered with the water and vinegar. Cover with plastic wrap and let sit until ready to use.

2. To make the sliders, in a large bowl, using your hands, mix together the pork, chili garlic sauce, fish sauce, lime juice, and sugar until evenly combined. Shape into 12 even 2-inch-wide patties and place on a baking sheet. Brush both sides with oil and let sit for 15 minutes.

3. Heat an outdoor grill or stovetop grill pan over medium-high heat. Grill the sliders for 4 minutes, flip over, and continue to cook until an instant-read thermometer reads 145°F, about 3 minutes. Transfer to a large platter or baking sheet and let rest for 5 minutes.

4. To assemble the sliders, cut the rolls in half and spread each half with some aioli. Add a pork slider to the bottom half of each roll, followed by a handful of the pickled vegetables, a few slices of cucumber, jalapeño, and cilantro. Divide the ham slices evenly among the sliders and then replace the top half of the rolls. Skewer with a long toothpick to hold in place, and serve immediately.

taco sliders

2 teaspoons chili powder

1½ teaspoons ground cumin

1 teaspoon plus a pinch of kosher salt

1 teaspoon plus a pinch of coarsely ground black pepper

½ teaspoon garlic powder

½ teaspoon onion powder

½ teaspoon paprika

¼ teaspoon dried crushed red pepper

¼ teaspoon dried oregano

2 pounds ground beef (80 percent lean and 20 percent fat)

1 tablespoon olive oil

2 ripe large avocados, pitted and peeled

Juice from 1 lime

12 Braided Challah Buns (page 140) or store-bought dinner rolls

Cilantro, Lime, and Green Chili Aioli (page 162)

1½ cups shredded cheddar cheese

1 small yellow onion, thinly sliced

3 medium Roma tomatoes, sliced

2 cups shredded iceberg lettuce

My name is Jonathan, and I'm addicted to tacos. There, I said it. I eat tacos at least once a week. They're easy to make, affordable, and are ready in a flash. Not to mention they go great with an ice-cold *insert any flavor here* margarita. Let's not forget about the chips and salsa. I also love guacamole. Did I mention I love everything about tacos? Taco Tuesdays will never be the same at your house again, thanks to these sliders. They're the new tacos. If you want to add another layer of flavor, instead of the chopped tomatoes, try a bit of store-bought salsa for that extra taco kick.

---

1. In a small bowl, mix the chili powder, cumin, 1 teaspoon of the salt, 1 teaspoon of the black pepper, the garlic powder, onion powder, paprika, red pepper, and oregano until evenly combined. In a large bowl, combine the ground beef and the seasoning mixture until evenly incorporated. Shape the mixture into 12 even 2-inch-wide patties. Place on a baking sheet and set aside.

2. Heat an outdoor grill, stovetop grill pan, or skillet over medium-high heat and brush with olive oil. Cook the patties on the grill for about 4 minutes. Flip over and continue to cook for another 6 to 8 minutes for medium-well. Transfer to a large platter or baking sheet and let rest for a few minutes.

3. Meanwhile, mash the avocados in a medium bowl with the lime juice and a pinch each of salt and black pepper, until somewhat smooth. You can leave them chunkier if you'd like.

4. To assemble the sliders, split the buns in half and spread each half liberally with some aioli and mashed avocado. Add a grilled patty to the bottom half of each bun, followed by some cheese, onion, tomatoes, and lettuce. Replace the top half of the buns and skewer with a long toothpick to hold in place. Serve immediately.

cuban sandwich sliders

YIELD: 12 sliders

2 pounds ground pork

6 tablespoons olive oil, divided

4 garlic cloves, minced

3 tablespoons fresh orange juice

3 tablespoons fresh lemon juice

1 teaspoon kosher salt

½ teaspoon coarsely ground black pepper

½ teaspoon ground cumin

½ teaspoon dried oregano

¼ teaspoon crushed dried red pepper

¼ cup finely crushed saltine crackers (4 to 6 crackers)

6 (4 by 4-inch) slices Swiss cheese, cut in half crosswise

12 Crusty French Bread Rolls (page 150) or store-bought crusty rolls

Roasted Garlic Aioli (page 162), or ½ cup mayonnaise

Sweet and Spicy Honey Mustard (page 170) or ⅓ cup Dijon mustard

12 thin slices Black Forest ham

½ cup pickle chips, drained

Sometimes, no matter what you do, you just need a small homemade Cuban sandwich right away—without having to wait hours for a pork shoulder to slowly roast in an oven. Who has that kind of time? These sliders are made with Cuban-inspired seasoned ground pork, and although they're not slow-roasted, they still have all of the flavors you love in a Cuban sandwich.

1. In a large bowl, using your hands, mix the pork, 3 tablespoons of the olive oil, garlic, orange juice, lemon juice, salt, black pepper, cumin, oregano, red pepper, and crackers until well combined. Cover with plastic wrap and chill in the refrigerator for at least 1 hour, and up to 6 hours. Shape into 12 even 2-inch-wide patties and place on a baking sheet. Brush both sides with the remaining 3 tablespoons of olive oil. Let sit at room temperature for 15 minutes.

2. Heat an outdoor grill or stovetop grill pan over medium-high heat. Grill the sliders for 4 minutes, flip over, and continue to cook until an instant-read thermometer reads 145°F, about 3 minutes. Place 2 pieces of cheese on each patty and cook a minute or two longer, until the cheese has melted. Transfer to a large platter or baking sheet and let sit for 5 minutes.

3. To assemble the sliders, cut the rolls in half and spread each half with the aioli and mustard. Top the bottom half of each roll with a pork slider, a slice of ham, and a few pickle chips. Replace the top half of the rolls, skewer with a long toothpick to hold in place, and serve immediately.

try these sliders with:

Braided Challah Buns (page 140)

Whole Wheat English
Muffins (page 142)

Classic Potato Rolls (page 154)

Chimichurri (page 168)

scotch egg sliders

Scotch eggs are a popular dish in the U.K., made by wrapping hard-boiled eggs in sausage, breading them, and then deep-frying. Sounds like a snack dream come true, right? I'm always up for deep-frying almost anything and everything, but I know that not everyone feels the same way. Something about deep-frying meat scares most people. Scotch eggs are so good though, that I didn't want you to not make this slider because of a fear of frying. So I came up with a baked version instead. Whipped ricotta, mashed peas, and kale (to make us feel like we're eating healthy) round out these pub-like sliders into a mouthwatering bite. If you're making these for breakfast, swap out the Italian sausage for breakfast sausage instead!

YIELD: 12 sliders

9 large eggs

1 cup all-purpose flour

1½ cups panko or plain breadcrumbs

Cooking spray, for greasing baking sheet

2 pounds ground mild or hot Italian pork sausage

1 cup ricotta cheese

2 teaspoons finely grated lemon zest

2 tablespoons fresh lemon juice

1. Place 6 of the eggs in a large saucepan, and fill the pan with cold water until they're covered by 1 inch. Set over medium heat and bring to a full boil. Cover, remove from the heat, and let sit for 15 minutes. Pour out the warm water and fill the pan with cold water until the eggs have cooled down. Give each egg a gentle tap to crack the shells, and peel completely. Then rinse off with water.

2. Crack the 3 remaining eggs into a shallow dish and whisk. Pour the flour into a separate shallow dish and the breadcrumbs into a third dish.

3. Preheat the oven to 400°F. Line a baking sheet with aluminum foil and grease lightly with cooking spray. Set aside.

1 garlic clove, grated

1 teaspoon kosher salt, divided

¼ teaspoon coarsely
ground black pepper

2 (10-ounce) packages frozen peas

2 tablespoons unsalted butter

2 tablespoons milk

12 Whole Wheat English Muffins (page 142) or store-bought dinner rolls

4 cups loosely packed baby kale

Sweet and Spicy Honey Mustard (page 170), or ⅓ cup spicy brown mustard

try these sliders with:

Everything Bagel Slider
Buns (page 138)

Pretzel Buns (page 146)

Baked-Potato Buttermilk
Biscuits (page 156)

Sriracha Aioli (page 162)

4. Coat the peeled eggs lightly in flour. Divide the sausage into 6 even portions, and wrap each portion around an egg so that the egg is completely encased in sausage. Dip the sausage-coated eggs in the whisked eggs and then into the breadcrumbs, making sure to pat them well so they're fully coated in breadcrumbs. Place on prepared baking sheets. Bake until golden brown and fully cooked through, about 30 minutes total, flipping over halfway to evenly brown both sides. Remove from the oven and let cool slightly, then cut each egg in half.

5. Meanwhile, in a medium bowl, whisk together the ricotta cheese, lemon zest, lemon juice, garlic, ½ teaspoon of the salt, and the pepper until somewhat evenly whipped. Cover with plastic wrap and chill in the refrigerator until ready to use.

6. In a medium saucepan set over medium-high heat, bring the peas, ¼ cup of water, and ¼ teaspoon of the salt to a boil. Decrease the heat to low, cover, and simmer until the water has evaporated and the peas are tender, 5 to 7 minutes. Transfer half of the peas to a food processor along with the remaining ¼ teaspoon salt, the butter, and milk. Purée until smooth. Pour into a medium bowl, and fold in the remaining half of the peas.

7. To assemble the sliders, split the English muffins and spread each half with some of the ricotta mixture and the smashed peas. Place a few kale leaves on the bottom half of the muffins, then add half a Scotch egg and a tablespoon or so of mustard. Replace the top half of the muffins, and skewer with a long toothpick. Serve immediately.

hawaiian sliders

2 cups long grain rice, rinsed under cold water

2 (12-ounce) cans Spam

3 tablespoons low-sodium soy sauce

3 tablespoons olive oil

12 pineapple slices (about three 8-ounce cans), drained

12 Sweet Pineapple Hawaiian Rolls (page 152) or store-bought Hawaiian rolls

Sriracha Aioli (page 162)

I grew up eating Spam, and I'm not ashamed to admit that every once in a while I get a craving for it chopped up and served on top of white fluffy rice, with a drizzle of hot sauce (preferably Sriracha). I don't always give into the cravings, but when I do, it's definitely a treat that takes me back to my childhood because my mom made the best Spam and rice. Promise me you'll try this slider at least once before writing it off. You might end up loving it. Actually, I'm positive you will.

1. Bring 3⅓ cups of water to a boil in a medium saucepan set over high heat. Stir in the rice and bring back up to a boil. Cover, decrease the heat to low, and cook for 20 minutes without removing the lid. Remove from the heat and let sit for 10 minutes, untouched.

2. Slice the Spam into ½-inch-thick slices and arrange on a baking sheet. Brush both sides evenly with about half of the soy sauce and olive oil. Arrange the pineapple slices on a separate baking sheet and brush both sides with the remaining soy sauce and olive oil. Set a stovetop grill pan over medium-high heat. Grill the Spam slices on both sides until crispy, 5 to 7 minutes total, flipping over once. Transfer to a large platter or baking sheet. Grill the pineapple slices in the same manner, for 2 to 4 minutes total, flipping over once. If you don't have a grill pan, you can sear the Spam slices in a skillet or bake under the broiler for a few minutes per side.

try these sliders with:

Braided Challah Buns (page 140)

Whole Wheat English
Muffins (page 142)

Classic Potato Rolls (page 154)

Barbecue Sauce (page 164)

3. Uncover the rice, and fluff with a fork. Using damp hands and a 2-inch round cookie cutter, shape the rice into 12 even patties. Place on a baking sheet.

4. To assemble the sliders, split the rolls in half and spread each half with some aioli. On the bottom half of each roll, place a rice patty, a slice of Spam, a slice of pineapple, and the top roll half. Skewer with a long toothpick and serve immediately.

western bacon cheeseburger sliders

YIELD: **12 sliders**

CRISPY ONION RINGS

1 cup all-purpose flour, divided

1 teaspoon kosher salt, plus more for seasoning

½ teaspoon coarsely ground black pepper

½ teaspoon granulated garlic

½ teaspoon paprika or cayenne pepper

½ teaspoon baking powder

½ cup milk or water

1 large egg, lightly beaten

1 large Vidalia onion, thinly sliced into rings

Canola or vegetable oil, for frying

I'm not above a simple cheeseburger topped with crispy onion rings and barbecue sauce every now and then. Sure, it's not white-linen-tablecloth fancy, but sometimes you just need to roll up your sleeves and get a little dirty . . . with barbecue sauce. Let's take off our top hats and tiaras, loosen our ties, and unbutton our top buttons because these sliders are taking us back to the basics. If you don't want to go through the steps of making the onion rings from scratch, use store-bought frozen onion rings instead. Just cook in the oven according to the package directions.

1. Heat about 2 inches of oil in a large, heavy-duty pot until a deep-fry thermometer reaches 360°F.

2. To make the onion rings, in a large bowl, whisk together ½ cup of the flour, 1 teaspoon of the salt, the black pepper, granulated garlic, paprika, baking powder, milk, and egg until smooth. Pour the remaining ½ cup flour into a shallow dish. Separate the onion slices into rings. Working with a handful of onion rings at a time, dredge in the flour, shaking off any excess, and then dip into the batter.

3. Set a wire rack over a baking sheet. Preheat the oven to 250°F.

4. Carefully place the battered onions in the hot oil, being careful not to over-crowd the pot, and fry until golden brown and crispy, about 3 minutes total. Flip over halfway through frying. Drain and transfer to a paper towel–lined baking sheet. Season with a bit of salt to taste. Transfer to the wire rack and keep warm in the oven while you prepare everything else.

continued on page 36

western bacon cheeseburger sliders

continued

SLIDERS

2 pounds ground beef (80 percent fat and 20 percent lean)

1 teaspoon kosher salt

1 teaspoon coarsely ground black pepper

2 garlic cloves, minced

1 tablespoon Worcestershire sauce

2 tablespoons vegetable or canola oil

6 (4 by 4-inch) slices sharp cheddar cheese, cut in half crosswise

12 slices bacon, cut in half and cooked until crispy

12 Pretzel Buns (page 146) or store-bought slider buns

Barbecue Sauce (page 164), or ¾ cup store-bought barbecue sauce

6 green lettuce leaves, cut in half

---

try these sliders with:

Everything Bagel Slider
Buns (page 138)

Braided Challah Buns (page 140)

Waffle Buns (page 144)

Sweet and Spicy Strawberry-Rhubarb
Tomato Ketchup (page 171)

---

5. To make the sliders, preheat an outdoor grill or stovetop grill pan to medium heat. In a large bowl, mix together the ground beef, salt, pepper, garlic, and Worcestershire sauce. Shape into 12 even 2-inch-wide patties and place on a plate or tray. Brush each side with oil, and place patties on the hot grill. Cook for about 4 minutes, turn over, and continue to cook for another 4 to 6 minutes, for medium rare, or 2 to 4 minutes longer if you want them well done. Place 2 pieces of cheese on each, along with 2 half pieces of bacon, and cook for a minute or two, so that the cheese melts. Close the grill or turn off the heat and transfer the sliders to a platter or tray.

6. To assemble the sliders, split the buns in half and spread each half with barbecue sauce. Place a bacon cheese slider on each bottom half, and top with a handful of the crispy onion rings, and a piece of lettuce. Replace the top half of the buns, and skewer with a long toothpick. Serve immediately.

mediterranean lamb sliders

2 pounds ground lamb

3 garlic cloves, minced, divided

4 tablespoons finely chopped
fresh mint, divided

2 teaspoons chopped fresh oregano

¼ cup loosely packed flat-leaf
parsley, chopped, divided

1½ teaspoons kosher salt, divided

¾ teaspoon coarsely ground
black pepper, divided

¼ teaspoon crushed dried red pepper

4 tablespoons olive oil, divided

1 cup plain Greek yogurt

1 small cucumber, peeled,
seeded, and thinly sliced

1 tablespoon fresh lemon juice

I find myself cooking a lot with Mediterranean ingredients, more often than any other. I like how you can make everything taste incredibly bright and flavorful with simple ingredients like fresh herbs, olive oil, yogurt, black olives, feta, and spinach. I make a big batch of Hummus (page 163) every Sunday, so that throughout the week I'll be able to use it in other dishes—like these sliders for instance. They have all of the Mediterranean flavors I love, and can be made without much effort at all. The lamb can be swapped out for ground beef, turkey, or pork, if you want to switch things up a bit.

1. In a large bowl, combine the ground lamb, half of the garlic, 3 tablespoons of the mint, the oregano, half of the parsley, 1 teaspoon salt, ½ teaspoon black pepper, and the red pepper until well incorporated. Shape into 12 even 2-inch-wide patties and place on a tray or baking sheet. Brush both sides of the patties with 2 tablespoons of the olive oil.

2. Heat an outdoor grill or stovetop grill pan over medium heat. Grill the lamb sliders for 5 to 6 minutes per side. Transfer to a platter, cover loosely with aluminum foil, and let rest for 5 minutes.

continued on page 38

mediterranean lamb sliders

continued

12 Braided Challah Buns (page 140) or store-bought slider rolls

Cilantro, Lime, and Green Chili Aioli (page 162)

Hummus (page 163)

1 small red onion, thinly sliced

½ cup crumbled feta

1 (8-ounce) jar sun-ripened dried tomatoes, drained

1 (2.25-ounce) can sliced black olives, drained

4 cups loosely packed baby spinach leaves

3. Meanwhile, in a medium bowl, stir together the yogurt, cucumber, remaining half of the garlic, remaining half of the parsley, remaining 1 tablespoon of the mint, ½ teaspoon salt, ¼ teaspoon black pepper, 2 tablespoons olive oil, and the lemon juice until evenly combined.

4. To assemble the sliders, split the buns in half and spread each half with the aioli and hummus. Place a lamb slider on each bottom half and top with a spoonful of the cucumber yogurt mixture, red onion, feta, dried tomatoes, olives, and spinach. Sandwich together with the top half of the buns, and skewer with a long toothpick. Serve immediately.

---

try these sliders with:

Everything Bagel Slider
Buns (page 138)

Whole Wheat English
Muffins (page 142)

Sweet Pineapple Hawaiian
Rolls (page 152)

Buttermilk Ranch Dressing (page 170)

CLASSIC TURKEY CLUB SLIDERS 42
BUTTERMILK FRIED CHICKEN AND WAFFLE SLIDERS 45
BUFFALO CHICKEN SLIDERS 47
THANKSGIVING SLIDERS 50
CHICKEN BACON RANCH SLIDERS 52
TURKEY MEATLOAF SLIDERS 55
CHICKEN PARMESAN SLIDERS 57
ORANGE CHICKEN SLIDERS 60
TURKEY-BACON BLT AVOCADO SLIDERS 63
CHICKEN CURRY SLIDERS 64
SHREDDED BBQ CHICKEN SLIDERS 66
GRILLED CHICKEN PESTO PANINI SLIDERS 69
ROAST CHICKEN SALAD SLIDERS 70

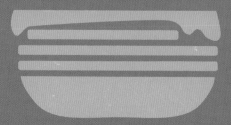

chapter 3

poultry sliders

I find that poultry lends itself to being adapted rather easily. Chicken happens to be my go-to protein when I cook at home because I can make it a thousand different ways, and I know that each time will be vastly different than the one before. It's like a sponge that can absorb a lot of flavor without any effort at all. However, there's no reason we should be stuck in a rut, making the same baked lemon rosemary chicken week after week.

With only a handful of simple ingredients like grilled chicken, Arugula Pumpkin Seed Pesto (page 167), mozzarella cheese, and roasted red peppers,

we can make something intricate in flavor, like Grilled Chicken Pesto Panini Sliders (page 69), which are sure to wow a crowd. Soft Rosemary Parmesan Focaccia Buns (page 148) are the perfect vessel to hold everything in place; a trip to the panini press takes them to the next level. Whether you're looking for new and exciting easy-to-make chicken or turkey slider recipes (see Orange Chicken Sliders, page 60), or you're on the search for classic dishes that remind you of your childhood (see Turkey Meatloaf Sliders, page 55), there are plenty of delicious options in this chapter to choose from.

classic turkey club sliders

YIELD: **12 sliders**

1 (2½ to 3-pound) turkey breast, bone-in and skin-on

4 tablespoons unsalted butter, softened

1½ teaspoons kosher salt

¾ teaspoon coarsely ground black pepper

1 teaspoon chopped fresh thyme

1 teaspoon chopped fresh rosemary

2 garlic cloves, grated

12 Whole Wheat English Muffins (page 142) or store-bought slider buns

Roasted Garlic Aioli (page 162)

12 slices bacon, cooked until crispy

6 (4 by 4-inch) slices cheddar cheese, cut in half crosswise

6 iceberg lettuce leaves, cut in half

3 medium tomatoes, sliced

In order to have the best club sandwich sliders, you need to roast your own turkey breast. Sure, it might seem like a lot of work, and yeah, maybe it's easier to go to the deli counter and order slices of turkey there, but would it taste as great as if you were to do it yourself? The answer is no. Good news for you is that the turkey can be roasted up to four days in advance, sliced, and kept in the fridge in an airtight container until ready to use. Even better news is that this recipe is perfect for all those Thanksgiving Day leftovers. Talk about saving yourself some time. Also, feel free to swap out the bacon for turkey bacon in this recipe, if you want to keep things pork-free.

1. Preheat the oven to 425°F. Line a rimmed baking sheet with aluminum foil and place the turkey breast on it. Using your hands, spread the softened butter under the turkey skin as best you can. Sprinkle the top with the salt, pepper, thyme, rosemary, and garlic.

2. Roast the turkey breast, skin side up, on the baking sheet until the skin is crisp and golden brown and an instant-read thermometer registers 165°F, 45 to 55 minutes. Every 10 minutes, baste the top of the turkey breast with the pan juices. Transfer to a cutting board and let rest for at least 10 minutes before slicing.

3. To assemble the sliders, split and toast the English muffins. Spread both halves with aioli and then top with turkey slices, bacon, cheese, lettuce, and tomato. Sandwich both halves together and skewer with a long toothpick to hold in place. Serve immediately.

try these sliders with:

Everything Bagel Slider
Buns (page 138)

Rosemary Parmesan Focaccia
Buns (page 148)

Crusty French Bread Rolls (page 150)

Arugula Pumpkin Seed
Pesto (page 167)

buttermilk fried chicken and waffle sliders

YIELD: **12 sliders**

4 (6 to 8-ounce) skinless boneless chicken breasts

½ medium yellow onion, sliced

2 garlic cloves, smashed and peeled

½ cup pickled jalapeño juice

1½ teaspoons kosher salt, divided

1½ teaspoons coarsely ground black pepper, divided

2 cups all-purpose flour

½ teaspoon paprika

½ teaspoon ground thyme

½ teaspoon granulated onion

½ teaspoon granulated garlic

3 cups buttermilk, divided (see Note)

Canola oil, for frying

The most popular post on my blog is a fried chicken and waffle sandwich. I had no idea it would become so big when I originally wrote it, but when you stop and really think about it, what's not to like? Crispy buttermilk fried chicken, lettuce, avocado, tomato, and a honey mustard sauce sandwiched between crispy waffles that are loaded with cheddar, bacon, and scallions. I'm positive these ingredients are what dreams are made of. And just when you thought it couldn't get any better, now it's in a slider form, which basically just gives you the right to eat more than your fair share. They're small—live a little!

If you're not a fan of spicy, you can skip the pickled jalapeño juice brine, and brine the chicken in the buttermilk instead for the same amount of time.

---

1. Cut each chicken breast into 3 pieces, so you end up with 12 pieces, and place in a large mixing bowl. Add the onion, garlic, jalapeño juice, ½ teaspoon of the salt, and ½ teaspoon of the pepper to the chicken. Mix until evenly combined and well coated or place the chicken in 1½ cups of the buttermilk if you're not using brine. Cover tightly with plastic wrap and let chill in the refrigerator for 4 to 6 hours.

2. In a shallow dish, whisk together the flour, remaining teaspoon of salt, remaining teaspoon of pepper, the paprika, thyme, granulated onion, and granulated garlic. Pour the remaining 1½ cups buttermilk in a separate shallow dish.

continued on page 46

buttermilk fried chicken and waffle sliders

continued

Sweet and Spicy Honey
Mustard (page 170)

12 Waffle Buns (page 144), or 6 frozen
Belgian waffles cut into quarters

6 lettuce leaves, cut in half

3 medium tomatoes, sliced

2 ripe medium avocados,
pitted, peeled, and sliced

12 pieces bacon, cut in half
and cooked until crispy

try these sliders with:

Braided Challah Buns (page 140)

Sweet Pineapple Hawaiian
Rolls (page 152)

Black Pepper Buttermilk
Biscuits (page 145)

Sriracha Aioli (page 162)

3. Set a wire rack over a baking sheet. To dredge the chicken, remove the pieces from the brine and dab them with paper towels to remove any excess liquid. Pass the chicken through the flour mixture first (shaking off any excess), then dip into the buttermilk, and once more into the flour. Place on the wire rack and continue dredging the rest. Let rest for about 10 minutes.

4. Meanwhile, set another wire rack over a baking sheet and preheat the oven to 250°F. Pour about 3 inches of canola oil into a heavy pot and heat until a deep-fry thermometer reaches 350°F. Carefully drop a few pieces of chicken into the hot oil with tongs, and fry until golden brown and crispy, turning halfway, 12 to 16 minutes total. Drain and place on the wire rack. Keep warm in the oven while you continue frying the rest of the chicken.

5. To assemble the sliders, spoon mustard onto half the waffles, and top with a piece of fried chicken, lettuce, tomato, avocado, bacon, and another waffle. Skewer with a long toothpick to hold in place, and serve immediately.

NOTE: If you are using the jalapeño juice brine for the chicken, you will only need 1½ cups buttermilk for the dredging process.

buffalo chicken sliders

YIELD: **12 sliders**

4 (6 to 8-ounce) skinless
boneless chicken breasts

1¼ cups buttermilk

¾ cup hot pepper sauce, such
as Frank's RedHot, divided

1 teaspoon kosher salt, divided

1 teaspoon coarsely ground
black pepper, divided

2 cups all-purpose flour

½ teaspoon paprika

½ teaspoon ground thyme

½ teaspoon granulated onion

½ teaspoon granulated garlic

½ teaspoon cayenne pepper

Canola oil, for deep-frying

Buttermilk Ranch Dressing (page 170)
or ½ cup store-bought dressing

1 cup crumbled blue cheese

3 tablespoons unsalted butter, melted

12 Crusty French Bread Rolls (page
150) or store-bought crusty rolls

4 carrots, peeled and cut
into 2-inch sticks

5 celery stalks, cut into 2-inch sticks

I always tell myself that I could totally enter a hot-wing eating contest, and that I'd win. Somehow, though, I get through about twelve wings and then I'm full. So I guess the "eating lots of food in one sitting" life isn't for me. Either way, I am a big fan of wings, and therefore I'm a big fan of these sliders. The crisp carrots and celery, and the cool buttermilk ranch and blue cheese dressing offset the spicy Buffalo fried chicken. It's the perfect balance of flavors. I'd most definitely enter a Buffalo chicken–slider eating contest. I probably wouldn't win, but I'd enter anyway.

1. Cut each chicken breast diagonally into 6 thin strips. Place in a large bowl and stir in the buttermilk, ¼ cup of the hot sauce, ½ teaspoon salt, and ½ teaspoon black pepper. Toss until fully coated. Cover with plastic wrap and chill in the fridge for at least 1 hour.

2. In a large bowl, whisk together the flour, the remaining ½ teaspoon salt, ½ teaspoon black pepper, the paprika, thyme, granulated onion, granulated garlic, and cayenne. Set aside.

3. Fill a large pot with about 3 inches of canola oil and set it over medium-high heat. Heat until a deep-fry thermometer reaches 350°F. Set a wire rack over a baking sheet.

continued on page 48

buffalo chicken sliders
continued

4. To dredge the chicken, remove a piece from the buttermilk mixture (allowing excess to drip off) and then dip into the flour mixture, rolling and patting to make sure it's fully coated. Place on the wire rack and continue dredging with the remaining chicken pieces. Let sit for about 10 minutes to allow the coating to stick. Preheat the oven to 250°F.

5. Fry the chicken in batches, a few at a time, until golden brown and crispy, for 5 to 8 minutes per batch, flipping over halfway. Transfer to a clean wire rack and continue frying the rest. Keep the chicken warm in the oven while you fry the rest of the chicken.

6. In a medium bowl, combine the buttermilk ranch dressing with the blue cheese; set aside. In a large bowl, stir together the remaining ½ cup hot sauce and the melted butter. Toss the fried chicken in the hot sauce mixture until fully coated.

7. To assemble the sliders, split the rolls in half and place a couple pieces of chicken on each bottom half. Top with a spoonful of the buttermilk ranch and a couple sticks of carrots and celery. Place the top roll on and skewer with a long toothpick to hold in place. Serve immediately.

try these sliders with:

Everything Bagel Slider
Buns (page 138)

Waffle Buns (page 144)

Pretzel Buns (page 146)

Cajun Rémoulade (page 166)

thanksgiving sliders

YIELD: **12 sliders**

TURKEY

1 (2½ to 3-pound) turkey
breast, bone-in and skin-on

4 tablespoons unsalted
butter, softened

1½ teaspoons kosher salt

¾ teaspoon coarsely
ground black pepper

1 teaspoon chopped fresh thyme

1 teaspoon chopped fresh rosemary

2 garlic cloves, grated

GRAVY

2 tablespoons unsalted butter

2 tablespoons finely chopped shallot

2 tablespoons all-purpose flour

1 cup chicken stock

½ teaspoon kosher salt

¼ teaspoon coarsely
ground black pepper

Thanksgiving is my second-favorite holiday—my all-time favorite is Fourth of July, but that's a story for another time—so it seems only fitting that a slider be made in honor of the runner-up. It features all of the flavors we love sandwiched together in a flaky buttery biscuit. If you're making these the day after Thanksgiving with all of your leftovers, feel free to add the leftover stuffing and/or green beans for that ultimate Thanksgiving leftover slider.

1. To make the turkey, preheat the oven to 425°F. Line a rimmed baking sheet with aluminum foil and place the turkey breast on it. Using your hands, spread the softened butter under the turkey skin as best you can. Sprinkle the top with the salt, pepper, thyme, rosemary, and garlic.

2. Roast the turkey breast, skin side up, until the skin is crisp and golden brown and an instant-read thermometer registers 165°F, 45 to 55 minutes. Every 10 minutes, baste the top of the turkey breast with the pan juices. Transfer to a cutting board and let rest for at least 10 minutes before slicing.

3. To make the gravy, set a medium saucepan over medium-high heat. Add the butter, let melt, and stir in the shallot. Cook until softened, about 5 minutes. Sprinkle in the flour and whisk until the flour is light brown, about 2 minutes. Slowly pour in the chicken stock, while whisking, and cook until the gravy thickens, about 15 minutes. Season with salt and pepper. Keep warm on low heat until ready to use.

SLIDERS

12 Baked-Potato Buttermilk Biscuits
(page 156) or store-bought dinner rolls

Roasted Garlic Aioli (page 162)

1 (14-ounce) can cranberry sauce

6 (4 by 4-inch) slices provolone
cheese, cut in half crosswise

2 cups baby spinach leaves

3 medium tomatoes, sliced

try these sliders with:

Braided Challah Buns (page 140)

Sweet Pineapple Hawaiian
Rolls (page 152)

Classic Potato Rolls (page 154)

Sweet and Spicy Strawberry-Rhubarb
Tomato Ketchup (page 171)

4. To assemble the sliders, split the biscuits in half and spread each half with some aioli. Spread a spoonful of cranberry sauce onto the bottoms of the biscuits and top with a few slices of turkey, the provolone, spinach, and tomato. Sandwich together with the top half of the biscuit and skewer with a long toothpick to hold in place. Serve immediately with warm gravy on the side for dunking.

NOTE: The Baked-Potato Buttermilk Biscuits (page 156) yield 9 biscuits, so you'll need to make a double batch for this recipe.

chicken bacon ranch sliders

YIELD: 12 sliders

4 (4-ounce) chicken breast cutlets

1 tablespoon olive oil, plus more for greasing pan

¾ teaspoon kosher salt

½ teaspoon coarsely ground black pepper

½ teaspoon granulated garlic

½ teaspoon granulated onion

½ teaspoon cayenne pepper

12 slices thick-cut bacon

1 small red onion, sliced

12 Black Pepper Buttermilk Biscuits (page 145) or store-bought biscuits

Buttermilk Ranch Dressing (page 170)

2 small tomatoes, sliced

6 green lettuce leaves, cut in half

I had a life-changing flatbread at a restaurant once during happy hour, and I don't know if it was the Moscow mules clouding my judgment or it really was my taste buds reacting, but there was something about that super-thin-crust pizza that just made me fall in love with chicken, bacon, and ranch together. On their own, they are amazing, but combine all three and they're a dream team that can't be beat. In my opinion, they should never be separated.

1. Combine the chicken, olive oil, salt, black pepper, granulated garlic, granulated onion, and cayenne in a large bowl. For a more flavorful chicken, marinate in the fridge anywhere from 30 minutes to overnight. The longer it sits, the better flavor it will have.

2. Cook the bacon, in batches, in a large skillet until crispy. Transfer to a plate lined with paper towels to drain. Once cooled, cut each slice of bacon in half.

3. Meanwhile, heat a stovetop grill pan over medium-high heat. Lightly grease with olive oil. Cook the chicken for 2 to 3 minutes, flip over, and continue to cook for another 2 to 3 minutes on the second side. Transfer to a plate and cover loosely with aluminum foil. Let rest for about 10 minutes before slicing.

4. Grill the onion slices for 2 to 3 minutes total, flipping over halfway. Transfer to the plate with the chicken.

try these sliders with:

Braided Challah Buns (page 140)

Whole Wheat English
Muffins (page 142)

Crusty French Bread Rolls (page 150)

Barbecue Sauce (page 164)

5. To assemble the sliders, split the biscuits in half. Spoon about 2 teaspoons of buttermilk ranch dressing on the bottom halves of the biscuits. Top each with a few slices of chicken, 2 half pieces of bacon, grilled onion, tomato, lettuce, and another drizzle of ranch. Replace the tops of the biscuits and skewer with a toothpick. Serve warm or at room temperature.

NOTE: The Black Pepper Buttermilk Biscuits (page 145) yield 9 biscuits, so you'll need to make a double batch for this recipe.

turkey meatloaf sliders

YIELD: **12 sliders**

2 tablespoons unsalted butter

1 small yellow onion, diced

3 garlic cloves, minced

⅔ cup panko breadcrumbs

¼ cup whole milk

2 pounds ground turkey

1 large egg, lightly beaten

¾ cup Sweet and Spicy
Strawberry-Rhubarb Tomato
Ketchup (page 171), divided

2 tablespoons Worcestershire sauce

1 teaspoon kosher salt

½ teaspoon coarsely
ground black pepper

3 tablespoons Dijon mustard

¼ cup packed light brown sugar

12 Baked-Potato Buttermilk Biscuits
(page 156) or store-bought dinner rolls

6 butter lettuce leaves, cut in half

3 medium tomatoes, sliced

My mom was a big meatloaf maker when I was a kid. I think it's a requirement when you become a parent. "We're having a baby!" "Oh, yeah? Here, have this meatloaf recipe." It was one of my favorite things to eat, even though it took forever and a day to cook in the oven . . . or at least my mom's did because she wanted to make sure she dried it out as much as possible (sorry, Mamma). Now, as an adult, I'm making it out of ground turkey, trying to keep it as juicy as possible, and putting it between some biscuits with lettuce and tomato and calling it a slider. Don't try to fight it.

---

1. Preheat the oven to 350°F. Line a baking sheet with aluminum foil and set aside.

2. Set a small skillet over medium-high heat with the butter and warm just until melted. Sauté the onion and garlic until translucent, about 5 minutes. Remove from the heat and let cool for about 5 minutes.

3. In a large mixing bowl, combine the breadcrumbs and milk. Let stand for about 10 minutes. Add the ground turkey, egg, ¼ cup of the ketchup, the Worcestershire sauce, salt, pepper, and the cooled onions and garlic. Mix by hand until well combined. Use a large ice cream scoop to evenly portion out the turkey mixture into 12 balls and then shape into patties (see Note). Place them on the prepared baking sheet, giving them about 2 inches of space between each.

continued on page 56

turkey meatloaf sliders
continued

4. In a small bowl, combine the remaining ½ cup ketchup, the mustard, and brown sugar. Brush the mixture liberally on top of each meatloaf patty. Bake for about 30 minutes or until the internal temperature reaches 165°F on an instant-read thermometer. Remove from the oven and let rest for about 10 minutes.

5. To assemble the sliders, split the biscuits in half and place a meatloaf patty on each bottom half. Top with a piece of lettuce, a slice of tomato, and the top bun. Skewer with a long toothpick to hold in place. Serve immediately or at room temperature.

NOTE: If you don't have an ice cream scoop or just don't want to deal with the whole shaping of the patties, you can bake the meatloaves in a standard muffin tin. That way they're all the same size.

NOTE: The Black Pepper Buttermilk Biscuits (page 145) yield 9 biscuits, so you'll need to make a double batch for this recipe.

---

try these sliders with:

Braided Challah Buns (page 140)

Rosemary Parmesan Focaccia
Buns (page 148)

Classic Potato Rolls (page 154)

Barbecue Sauce (page 164)

---

chicken parmesan sliders

4 (4-ounce) chicken breast cutlets

1 teaspoon kosher salt, divided

1 teaspoon coarsely ground black pepper, divided

1 cup all-purpose flour

½ teaspoon garlic powder

½ teaspoon onion powder

¼ teaspoon paprika

3 large eggs

1 cup panko breadcrumbs

½ cup plain breadcrumbs

¼ cup grated Parmesan cheese

6 tablespoons olive oil, divided

Red Wine Marinara (page 169)

1 cup shredded mozzarella cheese

12 Rosemary Parmesan Focaccia Buns (page 148) or store-bought ciabatta rolls

¼ cup fresh sliced basil

You know that local Italian restaurant down the street in your neighborhood that you frequent far more times than you care to admit? It's just old Italian movie posters, red-and-white checkered plastic tablecloths, and signed photographs of Al Pacino covered in some form of chicken scratch that reads, "Thanks for having me, Don." You end up ordering chicken Parmesan because they offer "THE BEST" chicken Parmesan of any Italian restaurant and you end up loving it because it is in fact delicious. That's exactly what these sliders are—even Al Pacino himself would approve.

1. Cut the chicken cutlets into 2-inch pieces. Season with ½ teaspoon of the salt and ½ teaspoon of the black pepper.

2. In a shallow dish, combine the flour, the remaining ½ teaspoon salt and ½ teaspoon black pepper, the garlic and onion powders, and paprika. In a separate shallow dish, whisk the eggs. In a third shallow dish, combine the panko, plain breadcrumbs, and Parmesan.

3. Preheat the oven to 350°F. Set a wire rack over a baking sheet.

4. Dredge the chicken by first passing it through the flour mixture, then dipping into the egg and lastly, into the breadcrumbs. Make sure to pat down both sides to fully coat. Place on the wire rack and continue breading the rest.

continued on page 58

chicken parmesan sliders

continued

5. Place a large skillet over medium-high heat and add 3 tablespoons olive oil. Add half of the chicken pieces and cook for 2 to 3 minutes on the first side, or until golden brown. Flip over and cook for another 1 to 2 minutes. Transfer to a baking sheet. Remove the used olive oil and any crumbs from the pan. Add the remaining 3 tablespoons oil and cook the rest of the chicken in the same manner.

6. Spoon a tablespoon or so of marinara on top of each chicken piece. Sprinkle with mozzarella and bake for about 10 minutes to melt the cheese.

7. To assemble the sliders, split the buns in half and spoon a bit of the marinara on both sides of each bun. Top the bottom half of the buns with a piece of chicken, sprinkle with basil, and sandwich together. Skewer with a long toothpick and serve immediately.

---

try these sliders with:

Braided Challah Buns (page 140)

Crusty French Bread Rolls (page 150)

Classic Potato Rolls (page 154)

Arugula Pumpkin Seed
Pesto (page 167)

orange chicken sliders

YIELD: **12 sliders**

1 (6-ounce) package broccoli slaw

½ small red cabbage, finely shredded

Sriracha Aioli (page 162),
or ¼ cup mayonnaise

1 tablespoon sugar

1 tablespoon fresh lemon juice

2 teaspoons whole-grain mustard

1¼ teaspoons kosher salt, divided

¼ teaspoon coarsely
ground black pepper

4 (4-ounce) skinless boneless
chicken thighs, cut into pieces

2 tablespoons low-sodium soy sauce

2 tablespoons rice wine vinegar

1 garlic clove, grated

2 teaspoons grated fresh gingerroot

1 cup plus 1 tablespoon potato
starch or cornstarch, divided

Whenever it rains the only thing I want to do is lock myself indoors, open all the windows, grab a blanket, and sit on the couch while watching movies and eating takeout from the container. What do I normally order when I decide to eat greasy Chinese food in my pajamas? Thank you for asking. I always order orange chicken, steamed rice, and some kind of noodle. The noodles change from time to time, depending on my mood, but the orange chicken and rice always makes an appearance in my rainy day party for one.

---

1. In a large mixing bowl, combine the broccoli slaw, red cabbage, ¼ cup of aioli (or mayonnaise), the sugar, lemon juice, mustard, ¼ teaspoon of the salt, and the pepper until the vegetables are evenly coated. Cover with plastic wrap and chill until ready to use.

2. Place the chicken in a large bowl along with the soy sauce, vinegar, garlic, and ginger. Toss to evenly combine and let sit at room temperature for at least 15 minutes.

3. Set a wire rack over a baking sheet. Pour 1 cup of the potato starch (or cornstarch) into a shallow dish. Remove the chicken pieces from the liquid, letting any excess drip off. Slightly dust the chicken with the potato starch in the dish, shaking off any excess, and place on the wire rack. Let sit for about 10 minutes.

1⅓ cups fresh orange juice (from 4 to 6 medium navel oranges)

⅔ cup orange marmalade

2 to 4 small red chiles de arbol (optional)

Vegetable oil, for frying

12 Sweet Pineapple Hawaiian Rolls (page 152) or store-bought Hawaiian rolls

try these sliders with:

Braided Challah Buns (page 140)

Crusty French Bread Rolls (page 150)

Classic Potato Rolls (page 154)

Cilantro, Lime, and Green Chili Aioli (page 162)

4. Meanwhile, in a saucepan set over medium-high heat, whisk the orange juice, marmalade, red chiles (if using), the remaining teaspoon salt, and remaining tablespoon potato starch (or cornstarch). Continue to whisk until thick and bubbly, 2 to 4 minutes. Decrease the heat and keep warm.

5. Pour about 1 inch of vegetable oil into a large pot and set over medium-high heat. Once the oil is hot, fry the chicken in batches, until golden brown and crispy, 8 to 10 minutes per batch. Transfer the chicken to a paper towel–lined plate and cook the remaining chicken pieces. Add the fried chicken pieces to the pan with the warm orange sauce and toss to fully coat.

6. To assemble the sliders, split the rolls in half and spread each half with some aioli. Place a few chicken pieces on the bottom half of the rolls and top with a spoonful of the chilled broccoli slaw. Replace the top half of the rolls and skewer with a long toothpick to hold in place. Serve immediately.

turkey-bacon blt avocado sliders

YIELD: **12 sliders**

2 (6-ounce) packages turkey bacon

12 Everything Bagel Slider Buns (page 138) or store-bought dinner rolls

Sriracha Aioli (page 162)

Arugula Pumpkin Seed Pesto (page 167)

6 green lettuce leaves, cut in half

4 to 6 medium heirloom tomatoes, sliced

2 ripe large avocados, pitted, peeled, and sliced

try these sliders with:

Whole Wheat English Muffins (page 142)

Waffle Buns (page 144)

Crusty French Bread Rolls (page 150)

Buttermilk Ranch Dressing (page 170)

Turkey bacon is the unsung hero of bacon. It's the distant cousin no one really talks about, but they still secretly eat it. Eat the bacon, not the cousin, because that would be weird and creepy. Bacon is bacon, after all, and who can resist? Here, it's turkey bacon's time to shine. Pile it high between bread with tomatoes, avocado, and pesto for a healthier take on a classic BLT. Of course, if this still doesn't convince you or make a believer out of you, then regular bacon will work just fine in this recipe. We'll pretend it's turkey.

---

1. Place a few slices of the bacon in an unheated skillet. Cook over medium heat 9 to 11 minutes, turning often, until crispy. Transfer to a plate, lined with paper towels to drain off excess grease, and continue cooking the rest of the bacon.

2. To assemble the sliders, cut the buns in half and spread each half with aioli and pesto. Cover the bottom half of the buns with lettuce, a few tomato slices, avocado, and bacon. Replace the top half of the buns, and skewer with a long toothpick to hold in place. Serve immediately or at room temperature.

chicken curry sliders

YIELD: **12 sliders**

4 (4-ounce) skinless boneless chicken breasts

2 teaspoons kosher salt, divided

1½ teaspoons coarsely ground black pepper, divided

¼ cup canola oil

1 medium yellow onion, diced

2 garlic cloves, minced

1 teaspoon grated fresh gingerroot

1 tablespoon curry powder

1 teaspoon ground cumin

1 teaspoon ground turmeric

1 teaspoon ground coriander

1 teaspoon cayenne pepper

½ teaspoon dried crushed red pepper

1 (15-ounce) can crushed tomatoes, with juices

1 cup plain Greek yogurt

1 tablespoon fresh lemon juice

½ cup fresh cilantro leaves plus 1 tablespoon chopped fresh cilantro, divided

Those late-night trips to the local Indian spot—hoping you don't run into someone while in your pajamas—to pick up your order of curry and rice, so you can eat on the couch as you watch some TV, will no longer be needed. Make this simple curry at home and turn it into sliders so you can feel better about being in your pajamas while you eat dinner. Don't let the long ingredient list scare you off, half of it is just spices and seasonings, which are crucial to great-tasting curry. It is much like chili and soup: curry gets better the next day and the day after. So make the curry a day or two in advance for optimal flavor.

---

1. Cut the chicken breasts into large chunks and season with 1 teaspoon of the salt and 1 teaspoon of the black pepper. Toss to evenly coat.

2. Set a large saucepan over high heat and add the oil. Once hot, sear the chicken in batches until browned on both sides, 5 to 7 minutes per batch. Transfer the chicken to a plate or platter and set aside.

3. Decrease the heat to medium-high and add the onion, garlic, and ginger. Cook until the onion becomes soft and translucent, about 5 minutes. Stir the curry powder, cumin, turmeric, coriander, cayenne, and red pepper into the mixture. Add the tomatoes, yogurt, ½ cup water, and the remaining teaspoon salt and ½ teaspoon black pepper. Return the chicken to the pan and bring to a boil. Decrease the heat to low, cover, and simmer until the chicken has cooked through, about 20 minutes. Stir in the lemon juice and 1 tablespoon chopped cilantro.

12 Classic Potato Rolls (page 154) or store-bought dinner rolls

Cilantro, Lime, and Green Chili Aioli (page 162)

Spicy Pumpkin Chutney (page 165)

1 (15-ounce) jar roasted bell peppers, drained and cut into pieces

1 small red onion, sliced

1 medium cucumber, sliced

try these sliders with:

Braided Challah Buns (page 140)

Whole Wheat English Muffins (page 142)

Sweet Pineapple Hawaiian Rolls (page 152)

Hummus (page 163)

4. To assemble the sliders, split the rolls in half and spread each half with some aioli. Spoon about 1 tablespoon chutney onto the bottom half of each rolls and top with a few pieces of curry chicken, bell peppers, red onion, cucumber, and the cilantro leaves. Replace the top part of the rolls and skewer with a long toothpick to hold in place. Serve immediately.

shredded bbq chicken sliders

YIELD: 12 sliders

4 (6 to 8-ounce) skinless boneless chicken breasts

4 cups chicken stock or low-sodium chicken broth

Barbecue Sauce (page 164), or 1 (18-ounce) jar barbecue sauce

1¼ teaspoons kosher salt, divided

1¼ teaspoons coarsely ground black pepper, divided

1 (6-ounce) package broccoli slaw

½ small red cabbage, finely shredded

½ cup plain Greek yogurt

¼ cup mayonnaise

1 tablespoon sugar

1 tablespoon fresh lemon juice

12 Braided Challah Buns (page 140) or store-bought dinner rolls

Sweet and Spicy Honey Mustard (page 170)

½ cup pickle chips, drained

In my humble opinion, chicken should always be shredded, smothered in barbecue sauce, and topped with a creamy slaw. Of course, some sort of bread or roll should definitely be involved because we need a vessel to hold it all in place—we're not animals. These sliders are a combination of smoky and sweet, hot and cool, and they're perfect for summer gatherings with friends and family.

---

1. Place the chicken and chicken stock in a large pot and set over medium-high heat. Bring to a boil, decrease the heat to low, cover, and simmer until the chicken reaches 165°F on an instant-read thermometer, 10 to 15 minutes. Remove from the stock, reserving about 1 cup of stock, and let rest on a cutting board. Once chicken is cool to the touch, shred it with your fingers or 2 forks.

2. Pour the barbecue sauce, 1 cup reserved stock, 1 teaspoon of the salt, and 1 teaspoon of the pepper into a large saucepan and add the chicken. Stir until evenly incorporated. Set over low heat and cook until heated through, 10 to 15 minutes (see Note).

3. Meanwhile, in a large bowl, stir together the broccoli slaw, cabbage, yogurt, mayonnaise, sugar, lemon juice, and the remaining ¼ teaspoon salt and ¼ teaspoon pepper until evenly combined. Cover and let chill until ready to use. This can be made a day or two in advance.

try these sliders with:

Waffle Buns (page 144)

Pretzel Buns (page 146)

Sweet Pineapple Hawaiian
Rolls (page 152)

Buttermilk Ranch Dressing (page 170)

4. To assemble sliders, cut the buns in half and spread each half with some mustard. Place a mound of shredded chicken on the bottom half of each bun, followed by some slaw and a few pickle chips. Replace the top half of each bun, and skewer with a long toothpick to hold in place. Serve immediately.

NOTE: The chicken can also easily be made in a slow cooker. Place the uncooked chicken, 1 cup chicken stock, the barbecue sauce, 1 teaspoon salt, and 1 teaspoon black pepper in the slow cooker and cook on low for 6 to 8 hours or on high for 2 to 4 hours, until tender. Shred with 2 forks and assemble sliders.

grilled chicken pesto panini sliders

YIELD: **12 sliders**

4 (4-ounce) chicken breast cutlets

1 teaspoon kosher salt

½ teaspoon coarsely ground black pepper

½ teaspoon granulated garlic

½ teaspoon granulated onion

¼ teaspoon cayenne pepper

Oil or cooking spray, for greasing pan

12 Rosemary Parmesan Focaccia Buns (page 148) or store-bought ciabatta rolls

Roasted Garlic Aioli (page 162)

Arugula Pumpkin Seed Pesto (page 167)

1 (15-ounce) jar roasted bell peppers, drained and cut into pieces

1 cup shredded mozzarella cheese

---

try these sliders with:

Waffle Buns (page 144)

Sweet Pineapple Hawaiian Rolls (page 152)

Classic Potato Rolls (page 154)

Hummus (page 163)

For many years I begged Santa for a panini press for Christmas, and now that I finally got it, I use it all the time—I make only one kind of panini, though. Why mess with a good thing? I grill chicken and layer it with homemade pesto sauce, mozzarella, and roasted red peppers in focaccia to create the best panini you'll ever try. One night I had the genius idea of turning them into panini sliders. It was the best decision I ever made.

---

1. In a medium bowl, toss together the chicken, salt, pepper, granulated garlic, granulated onion, and cayenne until evenly combined.

2. Place a stovetop grill pan over medium-high heat. Lightly grease with oil or cooking spray and place the chicken on it in a single layer. Cook for 5 to 6 minutes or until grill marks form on the first side, flip over, and continue to cook for another 3 to 4 minutes on the second side. Transfer to a plate or platter and let rest for about 10 minutes before slicing into 6 to 8 thin slices.

3. Preheat a panini press. If you don't have a panini press just heat up a stovetop grill pan and toast the sandwiches on that. Place a heavy skillet on top with a few cans to weigh it down, and you'll be good to go.

4. To assemble the sliders, split the buns in half and spread about a tablespoon of aioli and a tablespoon of pesto onto each half. Layer with chicken slices, roasted peppers, and mozzarella. Sandwich together and place 3 or 4 sliders on the preheated press. Heat until the cheese has melted and the bread is crusty and golden brown. Serve warm or at room temperature.

roast chicken salad sliders

YIELD: **12 sliders**

3 (6 to 8-ounce) chicken breasts, bone-in and skin-on

¼ cup olive oil

2 teaspoons kosher salt, divided, plus more for seasoning

2 teaspoons coarsely cracked black pepper, divided, plus more for seasoning

4 sprigs fresh thyme

2 celery stalks, diced

1 medium shallot, minced

3 tablespoons finely chopped fresh parsley

3 tablespoons finely chopped fresh chives

1 tablespoon finely chopped fresh tarragon

1 tablespoon fresh lemon juice

½ cup dried cranberries

½ cup slivered almonds

Roasted Garlic Aioli (page 162)

12 Sweet Pineapple Hawaiian Rolls (page 152) or store-bought Hawaiian rolls

4 medium tomatoes, sliced

2 ripe large avocados, pitted, peeled, and sliced

6 butter lettuce leaves, cut in half

This is the slider you make when you want to have a light lunch or savory brunch with a couple of friends, while sipping on some iced tea (spiked or not—I won't judge) and talking about the latest episode of *Scandal*. It's also great for your book club meeting, a tea party on a Sunday afternoon, or a picnic at the park. For a more robust flavor, roast the chicken and make the salad a day or two before you plan on serving the sliders. The chicken salad is best when served cold, and the longer it sits in the fridge, the better. If you don't have time to roast your own chicken, a store-bought rotisserie chicken will work great in a pinch.

---

1. Preheat the oven to 375°F. Line a rimmed baking sheet with aluminum foil and place the chicken on it in an even layer. Drizzle and rub each breast with the olive oil and season with 1½ teaspoons of the salt, 1½ teaspoons of the black pepper, and the thyme sprigs. Roast in the oven until the juices run clear and the internal temperature reaches 165°F on an instant-read thermometer, 45 to 60 minutes. Remove from the oven and let cool completely.

2. Remove and discard the skin and bones from the chicken. Then shred or dice the chicken. Transfer to a large mixing bowl and add the celery, shallot, parsley, chives, tarragon, lemon juice, cranberries, almonds, ¾ cup aioli, and the remaining ½ teaspoon salt and ½ teaspoon black pepper. Toss to evenly combine. Taste and adjust the seasoning accordingly, adding more salt or pepper as needed. Chill in the refrigerator for at least 1 hour and up to 2 days.

try these sliders with:

Braided Challah Buns (page 140)

Whole Wheat English
Muffins (page 142)

Rosemary Parmesan Focaccia
Buns (page 148)

Cajun Rémoulade (page 166)

3. To assemble the sliders, split the rolls in half and spread each half with a bit of aioli. Place a scoop of chicken salad on the bottom half of each roll and top with a slice of tomato, avocado, and lettuce. Sandwich together with the top roll and skewer with a long toothpick. Serve immediately.

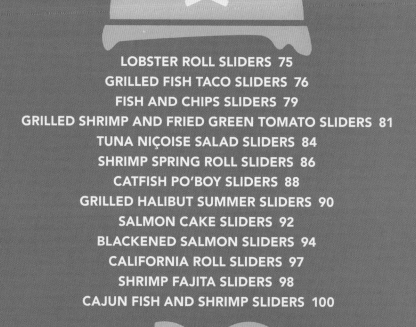

LOBSTER ROLL SLIDERS 75
GRILLED FISH TACO SLIDERS 76
FISH AND CHIPS SLIDERS 79
GRILLED SHRIMP AND FRIED GREEN TOMATO SLIDERS 81
TUNA NIÇOISE SALAD SLIDERS 84
SHRIMP SPRING ROLL SLIDERS 86
CATFISH PO'BOY SLIDERS 88
GRILLED HALIBUT SUMMER SLIDERS 90
SALMON CAKE SLIDERS 92
BLACKENED SALMON SLIDERS 94
CALIFORNIA ROLL SLIDERS 97
SHRIMP FAJITA SLIDERS 98
CAJUN FISH AND SHRIMP SLIDERS 100

seafood sliders

For some reason seafood just feels very fancy to me. If you're eating seafood you've made it big. You might as well just wear a sign that says, "I'm rich." Everyone will want to be your friend. Let me put it to you this way: Have you ever noticed how when you set out a seafood appetizer at a party—jumbo shrimp cocktail, hot crab dip, or dare I even mention bacon-wrapped shrimp?—those appetizers are always the first to go? People leave none for you, and practically wipe their plates clean. That's because people really love seafood. Seafood sliders are just what you need to switch up your traditional appetizer routine.

This chapter is the black tie of the book. It has all the components needed to impress your friends, family, and guests—delicious recipes, unique flavor combinations, and classic dishes turned into something worth writing home about. Some of my favorite restaurant dishes, like lobster rolls, tuna Niçoise, fish and chips, and California rolls, all get the slider treatment. Grab your friends and family; throw a party and step outside your food comfort zone. Try something new—I know you won't be disappointed.

lobster roll sliders

YIELD: **12 sliders**

1 tablespoon plus ¾ teaspoon kosher salt, divided

6 (8-ounce) lobster tails, thawed if frozen

½ cup Roasted Garlic Aioli (page 162) or mayonnaise

Juice from 1 medium lemon

¼ cup chopped celery (about 2 celery-heart stalks)

2 tablespoons chopped fresh parsley

½ teaspoon coarsely ground black pepper

12 Braided Challah Buns (page 140) or store-bought dinner rolls

4 tablespoons unsalted butter, melted

6 butter lettuce leaves, cut in half

try these sliders with:

Rosemary Parmesan Focaccia Buns (page 148)

Sweet Pineapple Hawaiian Rolls (page 152)

Classic Potato Rolls (page 154)

Cilantro, Lime, and Green Chili Aioli (page 162)

These sliders are probably the fanciest slider in the entire book, so put on those top hats and tiaras. Even though lobster is the most important ingredient in this recipe, you don't have to sell your arm, your leg, or your child in order to make these. The recipe uses lobster tails instead of whole lobsters for a more wallet-friendly dish without skimping on any of the flavor. These are also easier to make because you don't have to worry about cooking and breaking down whole lobsters. That's a fear we can overcome another time and day.

1. Bring 8 cups of water to a boil in a large saucepan. Add 1 tablespoon of the salt and bring back up to a boil. Add the lobster tails and simmer, uncovered, until the shells turn bright red and the meat is tender, 8 to 12 minutes. Drain and let cool.

2. Remove the lobster meat from the tails, chopping it into small chunks, and transferring it to a large bowl. Add the aioli, lemon juice, celery, parsley, the remaining ¾ teaspoon salt, and the pepper. Stir until evenly combined. Cover with plastic wrap and let chill in the fridge for at least 15 minutes.

3. To assemble the sliders, split the buns in half and brush each half with melted butter. Place a scoopful of the lobster mixture on the bottom half of each bun, and top with lettuce and the top half of the buns. Skewer with a long toothpick to hold in place. Serve immediately.

grilled fish taco sliders

YIELD: **12 sliders**

Finely grated zest and juice from 1 medium lime

2 garlic cloves, minced

1 teaspoon kosher salt

½ teaspoon coarsely ground black pepper

½ teaspoon ground cumin

¼ teaspoon cayenne pepper

4 tablespoons vegetable or canola oil, divided

4 (5 to 6-ounce) mahi mahi or cod fillets

Cilantro, Lime, and Green Chili Aioli (page 162)

12 Waffle Buns (page 144), or 6 frozen Belgian waffles cut into quarters

1 cup shredded green cabbage

1 cup shredded red cabbage

3 medium tomatoes, sliced

2 ripe medium avocados, pitted, peeled, and sliced

½ cup loosely packed cilantro leaves

Lime wedges, for serving

In Los Angeles, where I live, you'll find many restaurants that offer fish tacos on the menu. We know a thing or two when it comes to fish tacos down here in SoCal. They're either beer battered and fried until crispy, or grilled—as in this version— and can be made with a variety of fish or even shrimp. If you feel like being healthy, follow the recipe below. If you want to live on the wild side, you can take the beer-batter recipe from the Fish and Chips Sliders (page 79) and use that here instead. Either one will give you that same Baja California taco taste.

---

1. In a shallow baking dish, whisk the lime zest, lime juice, garlic, salt, black pepper, cumin, cayenne, and 2 tablespoons of the oil until evenly combined. Add the fish and flip over to coat both sides. Cover with plastic wrap and chill in the refrigerator for at least 15 minutes and up to 1 hour. You don't want to marinate more than 1 hour because the lime juice will break down the fish and change its texture.

2. Heat an outdoor grill or stovetop grill pan over medium-high heat and brush with the remaining 2 tablespoons oil, to prevent the fish from sticking (see Note). Once hot, place the fish on the grill and cook until the fish has loosened from the grill, about 4 minutes. Flip over and cook until the second side is white and opaque, 2 to 3 minutes more. Carefully transfer to a plate to rest for 5 minutes. Break the fish fillets apart into 12 pieces.

try these sliders with:

Braided Challah Buns (page 140)

Crusty French Bread Rolls (page 150)

Sweet Pineapple Hawaiian
Rolls (page 152)

Chimichurri (page 168)

3. To assemble the sliders, spread aioli on all the waffles. Place a piece of fish on half of the waffles and top with cabbage (both green and red), tomato, avocado, and cilantro. Sandwich together with another waffle and skewer with a long toothpick to hold in place. Serve with lime wedges on the side.

NOTE: Use a spatula to flip over and to transfer the fish to and from the grill. It'll make the process easier and prevent the fish from breaking. If your fish does break apart somewhat, that's okay. I won't say anything!

fish and chips sliders

YIELD: **12 sliders**

Canola or vegetable oil, for frying

2 large russet potatoes (about 1½ pounds), cleaned

3 cups all-purpose flour, divided

1 tablespoon baking powder

1 (12-ounce) bottle pale ale, cold

1 teaspoon kosher salt, divided

¾ teaspoon coarsely ground black pepper, divided

½ teaspoon granulated garlic

½ teaspoon granulated onion

¼ teaspoon cayenne pepper

4 (6 to 8-ounce) cod fillets, cut into 12 pieces

12 Pretzel Buns (page 146) or store-bought slider buns or dinner rolls

Roasted Garlic Aioli (page 162), or ½ cup store-bought tartar sauce

½ cup loosely packed flat-leaf parsley, chopped

Lemon wedges, for serving

Malt vinegar, for serving

After eating these sliders, you're going to start saying words like "blimey" and "cheerio." You might even have a British accent all of a sudden. These sliders are reminiscent of all those fun times you've had at the local pub, drinking a few beers and eating fish and chips. Now you can have that same pub experience at home. Beer-battered fish is topped with homemade fries and sandwiched together to create a slider that even the queen herself would approve.

---

1. Heat 3 inches of oil in a heavy-bottomed pot until a deep-fry thermometer reaches 350°F. Peel the potatoes and carefully cut into a thin julienne, about ⅛ inch thick. Rinse the cut potatoes in a bowl of cold water, and keep submerged in water until ready to fry.

2. In a large bowl, whisk together 2 cups of the flour, the baking powder, and beer until a smooth, thin batter forms. It should appear to be thinner than pancake batter. If the batter is too thick, add a bit of water or club soda to thin it out. Cover loosely with plastic wrap and let stand at room temperature for at least 30 minutes and up to 1 hour.

3. Meanwhile, place a wire rack over a baking sheet and set aside. Preheat the oven to 250°F. Lay a clean kitchen towel on a cutting board or baking sheet and place the potatoes on it. Dry them as best you can. Fry in batches until the potatoes are crispy and turn a nice golden brown, 2 to 3 minutes per batch. Place each batch of fried potatoes on the wire rack. Season with a bit of the salt to taste, and continue frying the rest of the potatoes. Once finished, keep warm in the oven while you fry the fish.

continued on page 80

fish and chips sliders
continued

4. Let the oil return to 350°F. Pat the fish with paper towels to make sure it is completely dry. Season both sides with a bit of the salt and black pepper. In a shallow dish, combine the remaining 1 cup flour, the remaining ½ teaspoon salt and ¼ teaspoon black pepper, the granulated garlic, granulated onion, and cayenne. Working with a few pieces of cod at a time, roll around in the flour, shaking off any excess, and then dip into the beer batter. Carefully place into the hot oil. Fry each batch of fish until golden brown and crispy on both sides, 2 to 3 minutes per batch. Drain on paper towels, and continue frying the rest of the fish.

5. To assemble sliders, split the buns in half, and spread each half with aioli. Place a piece of fried fish on the bottom half of the buns, and top with a small handful of fried potatoes. Sprinkle with parsley, and sandwich together with the top half of the buns. Skewer with a long toothpick to hold in place. Serve with lemon wedges and malt vinegar on the side.

try these sliders with:

Everything Bagel Slider
Buns (page 138)

Braided Challah Buns (page 140)

Crusty French Bread Rolls (page 150)

Cajun Rémoulade (page 166)

grilled shrimp and fried green tomato sliders

YIELD: **12 sliders**

12 large shrimp (20 to 25 count), peeled and deveined

1 tablespoon olive oil

¼ teaspoon Old Bay Seasoning

¾ teaspoon paprika, divided

¾ teaspoon cayenne pepper, divided

Cooking spray or vegetable oil, for greasing pan

4 green tomatoes, cut into ¼-inch slices

1 teaspoon plus a pinch kosher salt

1 teaspoon plus a pinch coarsely ground black pepper

1 cup all-purpose flour

2 teaspoons garlic powder

1½ cups panko breadcrumbs

4 large eggs

2 tablespoons whole milk

1 cup vegetable or canola oil, for frying

12 Braided Challah Buns (page 140) or store-bought dinner rolls

Cajun Rémoulade sauce (page 166)

6 green lettuce leaves, cut in half

½ cup pickle chips, drained

If you've been keeping track, you'll have noticed by now that there are quite a few New Orleans–inspired sliders in this chapter. That's because I've never been more fascinated by a city's food scene than with NOLA's. The focus on fresh local ingredients like seafood, the love they put into their dishes, and the passion of an incredible city rich in history come through in all of their food. Although they're famous for such dishes as jambalaya and gumbo, their fried green tomatoes and shrimp rémoulade are very near and dear to me. These sliders are the epitome of a New Orleans slider . . . if the city had its own slider.

1. In a large bowl, toss together the shrimp, olive oil, Old Bay Seasoning, ¼ teaspoon of the paprika, and ¼ teaspoon of the cayenne until evenly coated. Heat a stovetop grill pan over medium-high heat. Grease with cooking spray or oil. Once hot, lay out the shrimp in a single layer. Cook for 2 to 4 minutes on the first side, or until charred and bright pink. Turn over and cook for another 1 to 2 minutes. Transfer to a plate or platter and set aside.

continued on page 83

grilled shrimp and fried green tomato sliders

continued

2. Lay the tomato slices in a single layer on a baking sheet. Season both sides with 1 teaspoon of the salt and 1 teaspoon of the black pepper. In a shallow dish, combine the flour, garlic powder, and a pinch each of salt and pepper. In a separate shallow dish, combine the breadcrumbs, the remaining ½ teaspoon paprika, and remaining ½ teaspoon cayenne. In a third bowl, whisk together the eggs and milk.

3. Set a wire rack over a baking sheet. Coat the tomato slices first in the flour mixture, dredging both sides and shaking off any excess. Then dip into the egg and finally into the breadcrumb mixture, making sure to coat both sides evenly. Lay the coated tomato slices on the wire rack and continue dredging the rest.

4. Set a large skillet over medium-high heat, and add about an inch of oil. Once hot, fry the tomatoes in batches for 2 to 4 minutes on the first side, or until golden brown and crispy. Turn over and cook for another 1 to 3 minutes.

5. To assemble the sliders, split the buns in half, and spread both sides with the Cajun sauce. Lay down a fried green tomato slice on the bottom half of each bun. Top with a grilled shrimp, lettuce, and pickle chips. Replace the top half of the buns, and skewer with a long toothpick. Serve immediately.

try these sliders with:

Whole Wheat English
Muffins (page 142)

Crusty French Bread Rolls (page 150)

Classic Potato Rolls (page 154)

Sriracha Aioli (page 162)

tuna niçoise salad sliders

YIELD: **12 sliders**

3 (8-ounce) fresh ahi tuna fillets

¼ cup plus 3 tablespoons
olive oil, divided

1 teaspoon salt, plus
more for seasoning

1 teaspoon coarsely ground black
pepper, plus more for seasoning

¾ pound green beans,
trimmed and cut in half

3 or 4 medium Yukon gold potatoes

12 Whole Wheat English Muffins
(page 142) or store-bought
slider buns or dinner rolls

Roasted Garlic Aioli (page
162), or ½ cup mayonnaise

4 hard-boiled eggs, sliced
into ¼-inch rounds

3 medium tomatoes, sliced

6 butter lettuce leaves, cut in half

¼ cup red wine vinegar

I've never been to Paris, but I imagine that these sliders are exactly what it would be like to go. They might even be better than taking a trip to France—who knows? Okay, so maybe not better than the real thing, but perhaps a close second. The classic French salad gets a slider makeover, and if you're like me and have never been to Paris, maybe it's about time we brought Paris to us.

---

1. Brush both sides of the tuna with 3 tablespoons of the olive oil, and season with 1 teaspoon salt and 1 teaspoon pepper. Set aside.

2. Bring a large saucepan filled with water to a boil. Add the green beans and cook until bright green, crisp, and tender, 3 to 4 minutes. Transfer to a bowl filled with water and ice to stop the cooking. Bring the water in the pan back up to a boil, and throw in the potatoes. Cook until fork-tender, 15 to 20 minutes. Drain in a colander, let cool, and then slice into ½-inch slices. Set aside.

3. Heat an outdoor grill or stovetop grill pan over medium-high heat. Grill the tuna 3 to 4 minutes on the first side, or until it no longer sticks to the grill. Flip over and continue to cook for another 1 to 2 minutes on the second side. Tuna should still be pink in the center. Transfer to a large platter or baking sheet and let cool for 5 minutes. Break into large chunks, or slice into ½-inch-thick slices.

4. To assemble the sliders, split the English muffins in half and toast lightly. Spread each half with aioli and place a few chunks or slices of tuna on each bottom half of the muffins. Top each with a few slices of hard-boiled egg, a potato slice, a few pieces of green beans, a tomato slice, and lettuce. Drizzle each with a little bit of the remaining ¼ cup olive oil and the vinegar. Season lightly with salt and pepper to taste. Replace the top half of the English muffins, and skewer with a long toothpick to hold in place. Serve at room temperature.

try these sliders with:

Pretzel Buns (page 146)

Rosemary Parmesan Focaccia Buns (page 148)

Black Pepper Buttermilk Biscuits (page 145)

Arugula Pumpkin Seed Pesto (page 167)

shrimp spring roll sliders

YIELD: **12 sliders**

1 (8-ounce) package rice
vermicelli noodles

12 Classic Potato Rolls (page 154) or
store-bought slider buns or dinner rolls

Thai Peanut Sauce (page 172)

1 pound large shrimp (21 to 25 count),
peeled, deveined, and cooked

1 cup fresh bean sprouts

3 medium jalapeños, thinly sliced

2 medium carrots, peeled
and julienned

½ English cucumber,
peeled and julienned

2 cups loosely packed fresh Thai
basil or Italian basil leaves

1 cup loosely packed fresh mint leaves

1 cup loosely packed
fresh cilantro leaves

I love getting appetizers whenever I go to a restaurant. There's something so awesome about a predinner snack before the main meal. You mean I get to eat something before I eat some more? Yes, please. I'm all about that life. One of my favorite appetizers is a Vietnamese spring roll. Mostly because I could eat about ten of them and still have room for dinner. If it's on the menu, I automatically get a couple of orders, eat them all at once, and then proceed to order dinner and maybe dessert. I immediately feel good about the series of choices I just made. If you want some variety in this recipe, swap out the shrimp for tofu or cooked chicken.

---

1. Bring a large pot of water to a boil and remove from heat. Add the noodles and let soak until tender, about 5 minutes. Drain the noodles, rinse under cold water, and set aside.

2. To assemble the sliders, cut the rolls in half and spread each half with peanut sauce. Dividing the noodles evenly among the rolls, place them on the bottom half of each roll, coiling the noodles into a circle so they stay in place. Set about 2 shrimp on each slider, and top with a few bean sprouts, jalapeño slices, carrots, cucumber, basil, mint, and cilantro. Replace the top half of the rolls, and skewer with a long toothpick to hold in place. Serve immediately.

try these sliders with:

Braided Challah Buns (page 140)

Crusty French Bread Rolls (page 150)

Sweet Pineapple Hawaiian
Rolls (page 152)

Sriracha Aioli (page 162)

catfish po'boy sliders

YIELD: 12 sliders

Canola or vegetable oil, for frying

1 teaspoon salt, plus more for seasoning

1 teaspoon coarsely
ground black pepper

1 teaspoon granulated garlic

1 teaspoon granulated onion

1 teaspoon cayenne pepper

1 teaspoon paprika

1 teaspoon dried oregano

½ teaspoon dried thyme

4 (6-ounce) catfish fillets,
cut into ½-inch strips

2 large eggs

1 tablespoon milk

1 cup all-purpose flour

1 cup fine yellow cornmeal

12 Crusty French Bread Rolls (page
150) or any store-bought crusty roll

Cajun Rémoulade sauce (page
166), or ½ cup mayonnaise

2 cups shredded iceberg lettuce

3 medium vine-ripened tomatoes, sliced

½ cup pickle chips, drained

Whenever I visit my friend in New Orleans, I try to squeeze in as many po'boy-eating opportunities as possible, and even though I always tell myself to pick a new type of po'boy, I inevitably end up ordering either the fried catfish or shrimp. I'm a creature of habit, what can I say? Speaking of shrimp, you can also make this with shrimp if you want to. Just swap out the catfish for two pounds of medium shrimp (peeled and deveined), and proceed with the recipe as directed. These sliders will make you feel like you're in the Big Easy, having the time of your life.

1. Fill a large pot or skillet with enough oil to fill just about halfway and heat until a deep-fry thermometer reaches 350°F.

2. In a small bowl, mix together 1 teaspoon of the salt, the pepper, granulated garlic, granulated onion, cayenne, paprika, oregano, and thyme (see Note). Pour half of the mixture into a bowl with the catfish strips and toss to evenly combine.

3. In a separate bowl, whisk the eggs and milk together until smooth. In a third bowl, combine the flour, cornmeal, and the remaining half of the seasoning mixture. Set a wire rack over a baking sheet.

4. To coat the catfish, pass through the dry ingredients, then into the eggs, and once again into the dry. Shake to remove any excess coating and place on the wire rack. Continue breading until all the fish is coated. Let sit for about 10 minutes to dry a bit. Preheat the oven to 250°F.

5. Fry the catfish in batches until golden brown, stirring constantly, 4 to 6 minutes per batch. Drain and transfer to a plate lined with paper towels to absorb any excess oil. Season with a bit of salt while hot, and place on another wire rack set over a baking sheet. Keep warm in the oven while you continue to fry the rest of the fish.

6. To assemble the sliders, split the rolls in half and spread each half with some rémoulade or mayo. Place 2 or 3 pieces of catfish on each and top with lettuce, a tomato slice, and a few pickle chips. Replace the top half of the rolls, and skewer with a long toothpick. Serve immediately.

NOTE: You can swap out all of the spices listed in the ingredients and use 2 tablespoons of Creole seasoning instead.

try these sliders with:

Braided Challah Buns (page 140)

Classic Potato Rolls (page 154)

Black Pepper Buttermilk Biscuits (page 145)

Roasted Garlic Aioli (page 162)

grilled halibut summer sliders

YIELD: **12 sliders**

3 medium ears fresh corn, shucked (see Note)

1 (15-ounce) can black beans, drained and rinsed

1 small red onion, diced

1 ripe medium avocado, pitted, peeled, and diced

1 small tomato, diced

¼ cup loosely packed cilantro leaves, chopped

3 tablespoons red wine vinegar

2 teaspoons kosher salt, divided

1¼ teaspoons coarsely ground black pepper, divided

½ teaspoon ground cumin

3 (6-ounce) halibut fillets

3 tablespoons olive oil, divided

12 Sweet Pineapple Hawaiian Rolls (page 152) or store-bought Hawaiian rolls

Cilantro, Lime, and Green Chili Aioli (page 162)

Chimichurri (page 168)

These sliders are dedicated to those last days of summer, when you're pleading at the world to make the sunny weather last just a little bit longer. You're not ready to say goodbye to the long warm evenings and fresh seasonal produce. Hold on to summer for as long as you can with these grilled halibut sliders topped with a refreshing grilled-corn and black bean salad. They can be made with any firm fleshed white fish, such as cod, tilapia, or catfish, if you prefer.

---

1. Heat an outdoor grill or stovetop grill pan over medium-high heat. Once hot, place the corn on the grill, turning often, until charred all around, 10 to 12 minutes total. Remove from the heat and let cool before cutting the kernels off the cob. Keep the grill hot for the fish.

2. In a large bowl, toss together the corn, black beans, onion, avocado, tomato, cilantro, vinegar, 1 teaspoon of the salt, ½ teaspoon of the pepper, and the cumin until evenly combined. Wrap in plastic wrap and chill in the refrigerator until ready to use. This can be made the night before; just omit the avocado and mix it in right before using (to prevent browning).

3. Brush the halibut on both sides with 2 tablespoons of the olive oil and season with the remaining 1 teaspoon salt and ¾ teaspoon pepper. Set aside.

4. Grease the hot grill with the remaining tablespoon of oil, to prevent the fish from sticking. Grill the halibut until the center is firm and opaque, about 4 minutes per side. Transfer to a plate or tray and let cool slightly. Cut into 12 even pieces.

try these sliders with:

Rosemary Parmesan Focaccia
Buns (page 148)

Crusty French Bread Rolls (page 150)

Classic Potato Rolls (page 154)

Arugula Pumpkin Seed
Pesto (page 167)

5. To assemble the sliders, split the rolls in half and spread each with aioli. Place a piece of halibut on each bottom half of each roll, and top with a spoonful of the corn and black bean salad. Replace the top half of the rolls, and skewer with a long toothpick. Serve immediately.

NOTE: If corn isn't in season, use a thawed 12-ounce bag of frozen corn instead. It'll still make for a great-tasting salad.

salmon cake sliders

YIELD: **12 sliders**

4 (6-ounce) skin-on salmon fillets

2 tablespoons olive oil,
plus more for frying

1½ teaspoons kosher salt, divided,
plus more for seasoning

1 teaspoon coarsely ground
black pepper, divided, plus
more for seasoning

4 tablespoons unsalted butter

1 small red onion, diced

3 garlic cloves, minced

1 small red bell pepper,
seeded and diced

1 small yellow bell pepper,
seeded and diced

4 celery stalks, chopped

¼ cup fresh parsley, chopped

1 tablespoon capers,
drained and chopped

1 tablespoon Worcestershire sauce

Couple dashes hot sauce

2 teaspoons Old Bay Seasoning

Everyone is always going on and on about crab cakes. It's "crab cakes this" and "crab cakes that"—everywhere I turn, there they are. "Crab cakes are so fancy. Crab cakes are so good." Do you want to know something, though? Salmon cakes are just as delicious and just as easy to make. Salmon cakes now have their own slider. Do crab cakes have their own slider? I don't think so. So next time you're throwing a party, try making these sliders instead. Everyone will be like, "Crab cake who?"

---

1. Preheat the oven to 350°F. Place the salmon fillets, skin side down, on a baking sheet lined with aluminum foil. Drizzle the salmon with the 2 tablespoons olive oil, and season with ½ teaspoon of the salt and ½ teaspoon of the black pepper. Roast in the oven until just cooked through and a bit firm to the touch, 15 to 20 minutes. Remove from the oven and cover lightly with foil. Set aside and let cool completely.

2. Set a large skillet over medium-high heat. Add the butter and let it melt. Stir in the onion, garlic, red and yellow bell peppers, celery, parsley, and capers. Cook for a few minutes until the veggies are soft, about 5 minutes. Season with 1 teaspoon of the salt, ½ teaspoon of the black pepper, the Worcestershire sauce, hot sauce, and Old Bay Seasoning. Cook a few minutes longer. Remove from the heat, transfer to a bowl, and let cool completely.

Roasted Garlic Aioli (page 162)

1 tablespoon Dijon mustard

1 cup plain breadcrumbs

2 large eggs

Olive oil, for sautéing

½ cup all-purpose flour

12 Everything Bagel Slider Buns
(page 138) or store-bought
slider buns or dinner rolls

2 cups spring lettuce mix

3 medium heirloom tomatoes, sliced

---

try these sliders with:

Braided Challah Buns (page 140)

Whole Wheat English
Muffins (page 142)

Black Pepper Buttermilk
Biscuits (page 145)

Cajun Rémoulade (page 166)

---

3. Separate the cooled salmon from its skin and flake into a
large mixing bowl. Add ½ cup of the aioli, the Dijon mustard,
breadcrumbs, sautéed veggies, eggs, and a bit more salt and pepper
to taste. Gently stir and fold, making sure not to break down the
salmon too much, until completely combined and well incorporated.
Cover with plastic wrap and chill in the fridge for at least 30 minutes.
Portion out the cakes and shape them into 12 even patties, each
about 2 inches in diameter.

4. Preheat the oven to 250°F. Set a large skillet over medium-high
heat and add enough olive oil to cover the bottom. Dredge the salmon
cakes in flour, shaking off the excess, and place in the hot oil. Sauté
for 2 to 4 minutes per side, until golden brown and crispy. Transfer
to a baking sheet and keep warm in the oven until ready to eat.

5. To assemble the sliders, split the buns in half, and spread each
half with aioli. Place a salmon cake on the bottom half of each bun,
and top with lettuce and tomato. Replace the top half of each bun,
and skewer with a long toothpick to hold in place. Serve immediately.

blackened salmon sliders

2 tablespoons ground paprika

1 tablespoon cayenne pepper

1 tablespoon onion powder

1 tablespoon garlic powder

2 teaspoons kosher salt

1 teaspoon coarsely
ground black pepper

¼ teaspoon dried thyme

¼ teaspoon dried basil

¼ teaspoon dried oregano

4 (6 to 7-ounce) salmon fillets,
skinned and deboned

¼ cup olive oil, divided

12 Black Pepper Buttermilk Biscuits
(page 145) or store-bought biscuits

Roasted Garlic Aioli (page 162)

6 red lettuce leaves, cut in half

1 small red onion, thinly sliced

2 ripe medium avocados,
pitted, peeled, and sliced

3 Roma tomatoes, sliced

If you have a cast-iron skillet, now is the time to use it. Blackening is best when done in a heavy-duty skillet that can stand up to high heat. This is the slider you make to impress your friends and family. You'll go from slider maker to slider hero in no time. The seasoning mixture works great with all sorts of different seafood, such as tilapia, red snapper, mahi mahi, and even shrimp. (It's also great on chicken, but this isn't the poultry chapter so let's pretend I didn't just say that, wink wink.)

---

1. In a small bowl, mix together the paprika, cayenne, onion powder, garlic powder, salt, black pepper, thyme, basil, and oregano until fully combined.

2. Brush the salmon fillets on both sides with a bit of the olive oil. Sprinkle evenly with the seasoning mixture on both sides, making sure to fully coat both the sides.

3. Place a large skillet over medium-high heat and add the remaining olive oil. There should be enough to coat the bottom of the skillet; if not, add more until it does. Once hot, cook the fillets 2 at a time, until blackened, 2 to 5 minutes. Turn over and continue to cook for 2 to 3 minutes, until the second side is blackened as well. Transfer to a plate and let rest. Cook the other 2 fillets in the same way. Cut the blackened salmon into 12 even pieces.

try these sliders with:

Everything Bagel Slider
Buns (page 138)

Braided Challah Buns (page 140)

Sweet Pineapple Hawaiian
Rolls (page 152)

Chimichurri (page 168)

4. To assemble the sliders, split the biscuits in half and spread each half with aioli. Top each with a piece of salmon, lettuce, red onion, avocado, and tomato. Sandwich together and secure with a long toothpick. Serve immediately.

NOTE: The Black Pepper Buttermilk Biscuits (page 145) yield 9 biscuits, so you'll need to make a double batch for this recipe.

california roll sliders

YIELD: **12 sliders**

2 cups sushi rice or short grain rice

2 tablespoons rice wine vinegar

2 tablespoons sugar

2 teaspoons kosher salt

12 Classic Potato Rolls (page 154) or store-bought dinner rolls

Sriracha Aioli (page 162)

2 tablespoons sesame seeds

2 (8-ounce) packages flake-style imitation crab

2 ripe large avocados, pitted, peeled, and sliced

1 medium cucumber, peeled and thinly sliced

Wasabi, for serving

Low-sodium soy sauce, for serving

try these sliders with:

Braided Challah Buns (page 140)

Crusty French Bread Rolls (page 150)

Sweet Pineapple Hawaiian Rolls (page 152)

Cilantro, Lime, and Green Chili Aioli (page 162)

I'm slightly biased toward these sliders for obvious reasons. There are two requirements for living in California. You have to love avocados, and you have to eat sushi at least once a week; these sliders fit both of those requirements. Make them and, if you aren't already, you'll practically be a native.

1. Rinse the rice in a fine-mesh strainer, under cold running water, until the water runs clear. Transfer the rice to a medium saucepan along with 2 cups of water, and set over medium-high heat. Bring to boil, uncovered. Cover, decrease the heat to low, and cook for 15 minutes. Remove from the heat, and set the pan off to the side, covered, for about 10 minutes. Do not open it.

2. In a small saucepan, combine the rice vinegar, sugar, and salt. Place over medium-low heat and cook just until warm to the touch, 1 to 2 minutes.

3. Uncover the rice, and fluff with a fork. Transfer to a large glass or wooden bowl and add the vinegar mixture. Gently fold with a rubber spatula to thoroughly combine and coat the rice with the mixture. Let cool to room temperature. Using damp hands, and a 2-inch round cookie cutter, shape the rice into 12 even patties. Place on a baking sheet.

4. To assemble the sliders, split the rolls in half and spread each half with aioli. Place a rice patty on the bottom half of each roll. Top with a few sesame seeds, some imitation crab, avocado, and cucumber. Replace the top half of the rolls, and skewer with a long toothpick to hold in place. Serve immediately with wasabi and soy sauce for dipping.

shrimp fajita sliders

YIELD: **12 sliders**

1 pound large uncooked shrimp (21 to 25 count), peeled and deveined

1 teaspoon kosher salt, divided

1 teaspoon coarsely ground black pepper, divided

½ teaspoon ground cumin

½ teaspoon chili powder

½ teaspoon ground oregano

¼ teaspoon granulated garlic

¼ teaspoon granulated onion

2 medium limes, divided

2 tablespoons olive oil, divided

2 ripe medium avocados, pitted and peeled

1 (15-ounce) can refried black beans

1 small yellow onion, sliced

1 red bell pepper, seeded and sliced

1 yellow bell pepper, seeded and sliced

1 green bell pepper, seeded and sliced

12 Pretzel Buns (page 146) or store-bought slider buns or dinner rolls

Cilantro, Lime, and Green Chili Aioli (page 162)

¼ cup loosely packed cilantro leaves

You know how, when you go to a Mexican restaurant and order the fajitas plate, they come out sizzling with smoke billowing everywhere, and everyone turns to look at you, thinking you're so cool? These sliders are just like that, minus all the smoke and sizzling. They're just as cool though, and even more delicious because you made them! You can easily swap out the shrimp for grilled chicken or steak if you prefer.

---

1. In a large bowl, toss together the shrimp, ½ teaspoon of the salt, ½ teaspoon of the black pepper, the cumin, chili powder, oregano, granulated garlic, granulated onion, juice of 1 lime, and 1 tablespoon of the olive oil until evenly combined. Let marinate at room temperature for 10 minutes.

2. Meanwhile, in a large bowl, mash together the avocados with the juice of the other lime and the remaining ½ teaspoon salt and ½ teaspoon black pepper. Set aside.

3. In a medium saucepan set over low heat, warm the refried beans, mashing them with ¼ cup of water until smooth. Keep warm on the stove until ready to use.

4. Set a large skillet over high heat with the remaining tablespoon of olive oil. Once hot, add the onion and peppers. Sauté, stirring often, until soft and just beginning to caramelize, about 8 minutes. Stir in the shrimp and cook until pink and opaque in the center, 3 to 5 minutes.

try these sliders with:

Braided Challah Buns (page 140)

Sweet Pineapple Hawaiian
Rolls (page 152)

Classic Potato Rolls (page 154)

Chimichurri (page 168)

5. To assemble the sliders, split the buns in half and spread both sides with the aioli. Then spread the top half of the buns with the mashed avocado, and the bottom half of the buns with the warmed refried beans. Place about 2 pieces of shrimp on each bottom half and top with a few onions, peppers, and cilantro. Replace the tops, and skewer with a long toothpick to hold in place. Serve immediately.

cajun fish and shrimp sliders

YIELD: **12 sliders**

¾ pound catfish fillets

½ pound uncooked jumbo to extra-large shrimp (15 to 21 count), peeled and deveined

¼ cup sliced green onions (green and white parts)

1 large egg white

2 tablespoons chopped fresh parsley

1 tablespoon all-purpose flour

1 tablespoon mayonnaise

1 teaspoon Creole or Dijon mustard

½ teaspoon kosher salt

¼ teaspoon coarsely ground black pepper

2 tablespoons olive oil

12 Black Pepper Buttermilk Biscuits (page 145) or store bought-biscuits

Cajun Rémoulade sauce (page 166)

6 red lettuce leaves, cut in half

2 medium tomatoes, sliced

½ cup pickle chips

Making fish cakes at home is relatively new to me. I only discovered it recently, when I was really craving a homemade fish burger. Instead of going down the freezer aisle to pick up a pack of breaded "fish patties," I decided to be adventurous and try the fresh seafood case instead. Turns out, grinding up fish and shrimp with a bunch of other ingredients to make a mixture isn't all that difficult. The food processor does all the work for you. This slider is inspired by my trips to New Orleans. Catfish and shrimp are ground and formed into a patty, seared, and then topped with Cajun rémoulade sauce, lettuce, tomato, and pickles. Any white fish will work very well here—try cod or trout if you prefer.

---

1. Cut the catfish into small chunks. Place the catfish, shrimp, green onions, egg white, parsley, flour, mayo, mustard, salt, and pepper in a food processor. Process 6 to 10 times, until the fish and shrimp are coarsely chopped and the mixture looks like ground meat.

2. Line a baking sheet with parchment paper. Using wet or lightly greased hands, shape the fish mixture into 2-inch round patties, each about ½ inch thick.

3. Coat the bottom of a skillet with the olive oil and place over medium-high heat. Once hot, cook the fish cakes, a few at a time, until cooked through and golden brown on both sides, 8 to 10 minutes total. Make sure to flip them halfway through. Patties should be firm to the touch. Transfer to a platter and cook the rest.

try these sliders with:

Braided Challah Buns (page 140)

Whole Wheat English
Muffins (page 142)

Baked-Potato Buttermilk
Biscuits (page 156)

Buttermilk Ranch Dressing (page 170)

4. To assemble the sliders, split the biscuits in half. Spread the rémoulade onto the bottom of the biscuits and top with a fish cake, lettuce, tomato, and a few pickle chips. Sandwich with the top half of the biscuit and skewer with a long toothpick to hold in place. Serve immediately.

NOTE: The Black Pepper Buttermilk Biscuits (page 145) yield 9 biscuits, so you'll need to make a double batch for this recipe.

vegetarian sliders

Vegetarian recipes sometimes get a bad rap as being bland, unimaginative, and all-around undesirable. "Oh, you're vegetarian?! Here, have this salad." That's what I imagine a typical encounter is like between a vegetarian and a nonvegetarian. I'll be the first to admit that I've fallen victim to such thoughts once or twice. Simple salads might've even been involved. I've learned from my mistakes, though. I'm here to tell you and prove to you, as I'm sure many vegetarians can attest, that food without meat, poultry, or seafood isn't boring—or necessarily simple, for that matter. You don't even have to be a vegetarian to enjoy these; you may just feel like something lighter or healthier. Yes, sliders can in fact be healthy too!

These primarily veggie options, dressed with condiments like Sweet and Spicy Honey Mustard (page 170) or Spicy Pumpkin Chutney (page 165), are anything but boring. With flavorful ingredients such as vegetable tempura, roasted beets, curried cauliflower, and spicy tofu, these vegetarian sliders are just as tempting as their meat-filled counterparts. For instance, the Tex-Mex Black Bean Sliders (page 125) have all of the traditional taco ingredients in them, making it hard to miss the meat—while the Caprese Sliders (page 112) teach us that simple ingredients, like fresh mozzarella and heirloom tomatoes, are all that is needed to have a spectacular small bite.

bagel breakfast sliders

YIELD: **12 sliders**

4 tablespoons unsalted butter, divided

12 Everything Bagel Slider Buns (page 138) or store-bought mini bagels

1 (8-ounce) package cream cheese, softened

Arugula Pumpkin Seed Pesto (page 167)

1 small red onion, thinly sliced

2 medium cucumbers, sliced

4 ripe medium tomatoes, sliced

2 ripe medium avocados, pitted, peeled, and sliced

⅓ cup capers, drained

1½ teaspoons salt

1½ teaspoons coarsely ground black pepper

------

try these sliders with:

Whole Wheat English
Muffins (page 142)

Crusty French Bread Rolls (page 150)

Black Pepper Buttermilk
Biscuits (page 145)

Red Wine Marinara (page 169)

Weekday morning trips to the local bagel shop happen far more frequently than I care to admit, but that's only because I'm obsessed with bagels. So that's totally acceptable. I normally order an "everything bagel" loaded with all of the cream cheese the place has to offer (I'll eat them out of cream cheese, believe you me), and layered with so many fresh vegetables that they almost make it a healthy breakfast. These sliders are just like that, but so much better because you don't have to leave the house to get them. Your turn to host brunch? Set up everything as a slider bar and have everyone assemble his or her own bagel breakfast sliders.

------

1. Melt 2 tablespoons of the butter on a griddle or skillet over medium heat. Split the buns in half and place half of the bun halves, cut side down, on the melted butter. Cook for 30 to 40 seconds, until golden brown and toasted. Remove from the heat and repeat with the remaining 2 tablespoons butter and the rest of the buns.

2. Spread the bottom and top of each toasted bun with cream cheese. Top the bottom half of the buns with a spoonful of pesto, a few slices of onion, cucumber, tomato, avocado, and capers. Season with the salt and black pepper. Sandwich together with the top half of the bun and skewer with a long toothpick. Serve at room temperature.

mediterranean vegetable sliders

YIELD: 12 Sliders

2 (15.5-ounce) cans garbanzo beans, rinsed and drained

3 tablespoons olive oil, divided

½ cup fresh flat-leaf parsley

2 garlic cloves, smashed and peeled

2 tablespoons tahini

1 tablespoon fresh lemon juice

½ teaspoon kosher salt

½ teaspoon coarsely ground black pepper

½ teaspoon ground cumin

½ teaspoon cayenne pepper

1 large egg, lightly beaten

All the flavors of a gyro stuffed into a tiny package, without any meat? No, I promise it's not madness or a gimmick; it's just a slider. The homemade chickpea patties are packed with so much flavor that they'll make you forget you're eating a vegetarian dish. I think that's important for vegetarian cooking because we're trying to create something with as much flavor as possible. These sliders achieve just that.

---

1. Add the garbanzo beans, 1 tablespoon of the olive oil, the parsley, garlic, tahini, lemon juice, salt, black pepper, cumin, and cayenne to a food processor and pulse until coarsely chopped and the mixture comes together. Transfer to a bowl and stir in the egg and ½ cup of the flour until well combined. Shape into 12 even patties, each ½ inch thick. Place the remaining ¼ cup flour in a shallow dish and roll the patties in it, shaking off any excess flour.

¾ cup all-purpose flour, divided

12 Everything Bagel Slider Buns (page 138) or store-bought slider buns

Roasted Garlic Aioli (page 162)

Hummus (page 163)

1 small red onion, thinly sliced

1 medium green bell pepper, seeded and sliced

1 medium red bell pepper, seeded and sliced

1 medium cucumber, sliced

½ cup crumbled feta

1 (2.25-ounce) can sliced black olives, rinsed and drained

2. Heat the remaining 2 tablespoons of olive oil in a large skillet over medium-high heat. Cook half the patties at a time, until golden brown on both sides, 2 to 3 minutes per side.

3. To assemble the sliders, split each bun in half and spread each side with the aioli and hummus. Place a chickpea patty on each bottom half of the buns, and top with a few onion, bell pepper, and cucumber slices, the feta, and olives. Sandwich together with the top halves and skewer with a long toothpick to hold in place. Serve immediately or at room temperature.

try these sliders with:

Braided Challah Buns (page 140)

Rosemary Parmesan Focaccia Buns (page 148)

Crusty French Bread Rolls (page 150)

Spicy Pumpkin Chutney (page 165)

roasted beet sliders

YIELD: **12 sliders**

4 medium to large beets
(about 1 pound), rinsed

3 tablespoons olive oil, divided

2 tablespoons fresh lemon juice

1 teaspoon kosher salt

1 teaspoon coarsely
ground black pepper

12 Whole Wheat English Muffins (page
142), or store-bought slider buns

Hummus (page 163)

2 ripe large avocados, pitted,
peeled, and sliced

½ cup crumbled feta

8 ounces alfalfa sprouts
or baby arugula

True confession: When I was a kid, I was terrified of beets. The bright color and smell right from the can was a little off putting and scary, but it's one of my mama's favorite things to eat, so we always had them in the fridge. She'd place a few beets on top of white rice and call it a day. I, on the other hand, like them roasted and then grilled. To save yourself some time, roast the beets a day or two in advance. Peel and store in the fridge in an airtight container. Just slice before grilling and assembling the sliders. This is a great way to get non–beet lovers to change their mind—making the world love beets, one slider at a time.

1. Preheat the oven to 375°F.

2. Cut off the tops and roots of the beets and rub the beets with 1 tablespoon of the olive oil. Place on a sheet of aluminum foil and cover completely, making sure to seal the edges really well. Roast for 45 minutes to an hour, or until tender and easily pierced with a knife. Remove and let cool for about 10 minutes. Unwrap the foil and let stand until cool enough to handle. Peel with a paring knife or rub the skin off, and slice into ¼-inch-thick slices. Arrange on a baking sheet, drizzle with lemon juice and the remaining 2 tablespoons olive oil, and season with the salt and pepper on both sides.

3. Place a stovetop grill pan or large skillet over high heat. Quickly grill the beet slices, 1 to 2 minutes on each side, just long enough to develop grill marks; return to the baking sheet.

try these sliders with:

Everything Bagel Slider
Buns (page 138)

Sweet Pineapple Hawaiian
Rolls (page 152)

Classic Potato Rolls
(page 154)

Cilantro, Lime,
and Green Chili Aioli
(page 162)

4. To assemble the sliders, split the English muffins in half and spread each half with hummus. Place a few beet and avocado slices, the feta, and sprouts on the bottom half. Replace the top half of the muffins and skewer with a long toothpick to hold in place. Serve immediately or at room temperature.

fried zucchini sliders

YIELD: 12 sliders

½ cup all-purpose flour

1 cup panko breadcrumbs

½ cup plain breadcrumbs

¼ cup finely grated Parmesan cheese

2 tablespoons chopped fresh parsley

½ teaspoon dried crushed red pepper

½ teaspoon kosher salt, plus more for seasoning

½ teaspoon coarsely ground black pepper

What's a trip to your favorite diner or dive bar without an order of fried zucchini with buttermilk ranch for dipping? A trip not worth making, that's for sure. The way to do it is to convince someone to split an order with you, and then trick them into telling you a long story so they're busy talking and you're busy eating all of the zucchini. Now you can make your own fried zucchini and turn it into sliders, complete with buttermilk ranch for drenching and dipping to your heart's delight, all in the comfort of your home.

3 large eggs

2 large zucchini, cut into
½-inch-thick rounds

Canola oil, for frying

12 Everything Bagel Slider Buns
(page 138) or store-bought
slider buns or dinner rolls

Buttermilk Ranch Dressing (page 170)

3 medium Roma tomatoes, sliced

6 green lettuce leaves, cut in half

try these sliders with:

Braided Challah Buns (page 140)

Whole Wheat English
Muffins (page 142)

Waffle Buns (page 144)

Red Wine Marinara (page 169)

1. Measure the flour into a shallow dish. In a separate shallow dish, toss together the panko, plain breadcrumbs, Parmesan, parsley, red pepper, salt, and black pepper until well combined. In a third shallow dish, whisk the eggs together with 3 tablespoons of water.

2. Set a wire rack over a baking sheet. Dredge the zucchini slices first in the flour, followed by the egg, and then in the breadcrumb mixture. Place on the wire rack. Allow the dredged zucchini to rest for 10 to 15 minutes before frying, to make sure the coating sticks and doesn't slide off while frying.

3. Fill a large frying pan with about 2 inches of oil and set over medium-high heat. Heat until a deep-fry thermometer reaches 350°F. Preheat the oven to 250°F.

4. Fry the zucchini in batches, a few at a time, until golden brown, 1 to 2 minutes per batch. Flip over and continue to cook on the other side for another minute. Drain on a paper towel–lined baking sheet and season with a bit of salt while still hot. Keep warm in the oven while you fry the remaining zucchini.

5. To assemble the sliders, split the buns in half and spoon a bit of ranch onto each half. Top the bottom half of each bun with a slice of fried zucchini, a tomato slice, a piece of lettuce, and a drizzle more of ranch. Replace the top bun and skewer with a long toothpick to hold in place. Serve immediately.

caprese sliders

YIELD: **12 sliders**

12 Rosemary Parmesan Focaccia Buns (page 148) or store-bought ciabatta rolls

Arugula Pumpkin Seed Pesto (page 167)

1 (16-ounce) package fresh mozzarella, sliced

3 medium vine-ripened tomatoes, sliced

¼ cup sliced fresh basil

¼ cup balsamic vinegar

¼ cup extra-virgin olive oil

½ teaspoon kosher salt

¼ teaspoon coarsely ground black pepper

Let's talk about summer for a moment. When tomatoes are in season, you can't help but bump into them everywhere you turn. You'll feel the urge to buy every single one at the grocery store and the farmers' market stands. That's when you should make these sliders. If you can find ripe heirloom tomatoes in season, those are even better. The different varieties will not only provide various layers of flavor but also a pop of color. After all, we eat with our eyes first.

1. Split the buns in half and spread each half with pesto. Place a slice of mozzarella, tomato, and a bit of basil onto the bottom half of the buns.

2. Drizzle each with the vinegar and olive oil and sprinkle with a bit of salt and black pepper. Sandwich both halves together and skewer with a long toothpick. Serve immediately.

try these sliders with:

Crusty French Bread Rolls (page 150)

Sweet Pineapple Hawaiian Rolls (page 152)

Classic Potato Rolls (page 154)

Red Wine Marinara (page 169)

loaded baked-potato sliders

If I could eat potatoes every single day, I would. The fact that these potato sliders are sandwiched in a potato biscuit just proves that my love for this vegetable knows no bounds. This would be a great way to use up any leftover mashed potatoes you might have from the night before. Just shape into patties, dredge, and fry as directed. Although this is a vegetarian recipe, if you wanted to make these really "loaded," you could add a few slices of crispy bacon to each slider. Not necessary, but still very tasty.

YIELD: 12 sliders

2 pounds baking potatoes, peeled and diced

4 tablespoons unsalted butter

¼ cup buttermilk

1½ teaspoons salt, divided

1½ teaspoons coarsely ground black pepper, divided

1 teaspoon granulated garlic

1. Place the potatoes in a large saucepan filled with cold water. Bring to a boil over medium-high heat and cook until the potatoes are fork-tender, 15 to 20 minutes. Drain and transfer to a bowl. Mash with the butter, buttermilk, 1 teaspoon of the salt, 1 teaspoon of the black pepper, and the granulated garlic. Continue to mash until the potatoes are somewhat smooth. Set aside and let cool completely.

2. Once cooled, shape the mashed potatoes into small patties, using a medium-size ice cream scoop and damp hands to prevent the potatoes from sticking to your palms. Form into 12 patties, each about ½ inch thick. Let sit for a few minutes to firm up a bit.

3. Meanwhile, in a small bowl, whisk together the sour cream, chives, grated garlic, and the remaining ½ teaspoon salt and ½ teaspoon pepper, until completely combined. Set aside.

1 cup sour cream

1 tablespoon fresh chives, chopped

1 garlic clove, grated

2 eggs

1½ cups plain breadcrumbs

3 tablespoons olive oil

12 Baked-Potato Buttermilk Biscuits
(page 156) or store-bought biscuits

Roasted Garlic Aioli (page 162)

6 (4 by 4-inch) slices cheddar
cheese, cut in half crosswise

6 green lettuce leaves, cut in half

3 medium Roma tomatoes, thinly sliced

try these sliders with:

Braided Challah Buns (page 140)

Sweet Pineapple Hawaiian
Rolls (page 152)

Classic Potato Rolls (page 154)

Buttermilk Ranch Dressing (page 170)

4. Whisk the eggs with a splash of water in a shallow dish. Pour the breadcrumbs into a separate dish. Dip the potato patties in the egg wash and then dredge them in the breadcrumbs, patting them so they're fully coated. Place on a baking sheet and continue breading the rest.

5. Set a large skillet over medium-high heat and add the olive oil. When hot, cook the potato patties, in batches, for 2 to 3 minutes on the first side, or until golden brown. Flip over and cook for another 1 to 2 minutes to brown the second side. Transfer to a plate and brown the remaining patties.

6. To assemble the sliders, split the biscuits in half and spread both sides liberally with the aioli and the sour cream garlic sauce. Add a browned potato patty and top with 2 pieces of cheese, lettuce, and tomato. Sandwich with the top half of the biscuit, and skewer with a long toothpick to hold together. Serve warm or at room temperature.

NOTE: The Baked-Potato Buttermilk Biscuits (page 156) yield 9 biscuits, so you'll need to make a double batch for this recipe.

cauliflower curry sliders

YIELD: **12 sliders**

2 tablespoons canola oil

1 medium yellow onion, diced

2 garlic cloves, minced

1 teaspoon grated fresh gingerroot

1 tablespoon curry powder

1 teaspoon ground cumin

1 teaspoon ground turmeric

1 teaspoon ground coriander

1 teaspoon cayenne pepper

½ teaspoon crushed dried red pepper

1 (15-ounce) can crushed
tomatoes, with juices

1 cup plain Greek yogurt

1 teaspoon kosher salt

¾ teaspoon coarsely
ground black pepper

1 large cauliflower, cut
into medium florets

1 tablespoon fresh lemon juice

½ cup fresh cilantro leaves
plus 1 tablespoon chopped
fresh cilantro, divided

12 Classic Potato Rolls (page 154)
or store-bought dinner rolls

My oldest sister is a shopping-cart vegetarian. What I mean is she picks and chooses where and when not to eat meat. Once while visiting her house, on one of her "no meat days," she made a cauliflower curry dish with potatoes and peas that was to die for. So I vowed then and there to turn it into a slider, minus the potatoes and peas, because there's only so much I can stuff between a bun—but don't worry, all the flavor is still invited to the party.

1. Set a large saucepan over high heat and add the oil. Once hot, add the yellow onion, garlic, and ginger. Cook until the onion becomes soft and translucent, about 5 minutes. Stir the curry powder, cumin, turmeric, coriander, cayenne, and red pepper into the mixture. Add the tomatoes, yogurt, 1 cup of water, and season with the salt and black pepper.

2. Add the cauliflower to the pot and bring to a boil. Decrease the heat to low, cover, and simmer until the cauliflower is cooked fork-tender, 15 to 20 minutes. Stir in the lemon juice and 1 tablespoon chopped cilantro.

3. To assemble the sliders, split the rolls in half and spread each half with aioli. Spoon about 1 tablespoon of the chutney onto the bottom half of each bun and top with a few pieces of cauliflower curry, roasted bell peppers, red onion, cucumber, and cilantro leaves. Replace the top of each bun and skewer with a long toothpick to hold in place. Serve immediately.

Cilantro, Lime, and Green
Chili Aioli (page 162)

Spicy Pumpkin Chutney (page 165)

1 (15-ounce) jar roasted bell peppers,
drained and cut into pieces

1 small red onion, sliced

1 medium cucumber, sliced

try these sliders with:

Braided Challah Buns (page 140)

Crusty French Bread Rolls
(page 150)

Sweet Pineapple Hawaiian
Rolls (page 152)

Hummus (page 163)

eggplant parmesan sliders

YIELD: **12 sliders**

2 narrow eggplants

1 teaspoon kosher salt, divided

1 teaspoon coarsely ground black pepper, divided

1 cup all-purpose flour

½ teaspoon garlic powder

½ teaspoon onion powder

¼ teaspoon paprika

3 large eggs

1 cup panko breadcrumbs

½ cup plain breadcrumbs

¼ cup grated Parmesan cheese

6 tablespoons olive oil, divided

Red Wine Marinara (page 169)

1 cup shredded mozzarella cheese

12 Rosemary Parmesan Focaccia Buns (page 148) or store-bought ciabatta rolls

¼ cup fresh sliced basil

For the vegetarians ogling the chicken Parmesan sliders, have no fear, this one is for you. No longer shall you yearn for a hearty meatless slider that you too can enjoy. I've got you covered. I might love meat and poultry, but I can definitely also appreciate a vegetarian classic like eggplant Parmesan. The fact that it's in slider form just makes it easier to eat. It's important to find narrow eggplant, so that when you slice it, it fits in the bun. But if you can find only large eggplant, slice into rounds and then cut each round in half.

---

1. Cut off both ends of the eggplants, and then slice into ½-inch-thick slices. Spread out in a single layer and season with ½ teaspoon of the salt and ½ teaspoon of the pepper.

2. In a shallow dish, combine the flour, the remaining ½ teaspoon salt and ½ teaspoon pepper, the garlic and onion powders, and paprika. In a separate shallow dish, whisk the eggs. In a third shallow dish, combine the panko, plain breadcrumbs, and Parmesan.

3. Preheat the oven to 350°F. Set a wire rack over a baking sheet.

4. Dredge the eggplant by first passing a slice through the seasoned flour, then dipping it into the egg, and lastly, into the breadcrumbs. Make sure to pat down both sides to fully coat. Place on the wire rack and continue breading the rest.

continued on page 120

eggplant parmesan sliders

5. Place a large skillet over medium-high heat and add 3 tablespoons olive oil. Once the oil is hot, add half of the eggplant slices and cook for 2 to 3 minutes on the first side, or until golden brown. Flip over and cook for another 1 to 2 minutes. Transfer to a platter or baking sheet. Discard the oil in the pan, add the remaining 3 tablespoons oil, and cook the remaining eggplant slices in the same manner.

6. Spoon about a tablespoon or so of marinara on top of each fried eggplant slice. Sprinkle with mozzarella and bake for about 10 minutes to melt the cheese.

7. To assemble the sliders, split the buns in half. Spoon a bit of marinara on both sides of each bun and top with an eggplant slice. Sprinkle with basil and sandwich together with the other bun half. Skewer with a long toothpick and serve immediately.

try these sliders with:

Braided Challah Buns (page 140)

Crusty French Bread Rolls (page 150)

Classic Potato Rolls (page 154)

Spicy Pumpkin Chutney (page 165)

polenta and mushroom sliders

YIELD: **12 sliders**

1 cup whole milk

¼ teaspoon cayenne pepper

3 sprigs fresh thyme

3 teaspoons kosher salt, divided

1 teaspoon coarsely ground
black pepper, divided

1 cup fine yellow cornmeal

¼ teaspoon chopped fresh sage leaves

¼ cup mascarpone

3 tablespoons olive oil, divided

1 pound cremini mushrooms, sliced

Red Wine Marinara (page 169)

12 Rosemary Parmesan Focaccia
Buns (page 148) or store-
bought focaccia rolls

6 (4 by 4-inch) slices provolone
cheese, cut in half crosswise

I'm not Italian, but for some reason whenever I make polenta with sautéed mushrooms, marinara, and cheese, all of a sudden I feel like I can speak Italian. It's not a pretty sight to see, believe me. These sliders use homemade polenta cakes as the patty and are topped with browned mushrooms, red wine marinara, provolone cheese, and rosemary Parmesan focaccia. It's a classic Italian dinner in slider form. The polenta can be made two days in advance, stored in the fridge, and sautéed right before using.

---

1. In a medium saucepan, bring 2 cups of water, the milk, cayenne, and thyme to a boil over low heat. Season with 2 teaspoons of the salt and ½ teaspoon of the black pepper. Slowly sprinkle in the cornmeal as you whisk. Once fully combined, switch to a wooden spoon and continue to stir until the polenta has become thick. Let cook, stirring occasionally, until no longer grainy, 20 to 25 minutes. If the polenta becomes too thick before being done, add more water or milk, a little at a time, to thin it out. Discard the thyme sprigs and stir in the sage and mascarpone. Cook for a minute longer and then remove from the heat.

2. Line a 8 by 8-inch square baking pan with plastic wrap. Pour the polenta into the pan and cover with another piece of plastic, making sure that it touches the surface directly. Chill in the refrigerator for at least 3 hours.

continued on page 122

polenta and mushroom sliders

continued

3. Remove the polenta from the refrigerator and cut into rounds using a 2-inch circle cutter. Place a large skillet over medium heat and add 2 tablespoons of the olive oil. Sauté the polenta cakes, 6 at a time, until golden brown and crispy on both sides, 3 to 5 minutes per batch.

4. Place a separate skillet over medium-high heat with the remaining tablespoon of olive oil. Once hot, add the mushrooms and sauté until browned, 8 to 10 minutes. Season with the remaining teaspoon salt and ½ teaspoon black pepper.

5. Place the marinara in a small saucepan over low heat and cook until warmed through, about 5 minutes.

6. To assemble the sliders, split the buns in half. Spread the bottom half of the buns with marinara sauce. Top with a polenta cake, a slice of provolone, and a spoonful of mushrooms. Sandwich together with the top half of the bun and skewer with a long toothpick. Serve immediately.

try these sliders with:

Braided Challah Buns (page 140)

Crusty French Bread Rolls (page 150)

Classic Potato Rolls (page 154)

Sweet and Spicy Strawberry-Rhubarb
Tomato Ketchup (page 171)

tex-mex black bean sliders

2 (15-ounce) cans low-sodium black beans, rinsed and drained

½ medium yellow onion, chopped

2 garlic cloves, minced

2 tablespoons chopped fresh cilantro

1 tablespoon chopped fresh parsley

1 large egg, lightly beaten

1 teaspoon kosher salt

½ teaspoon coarsely ground black pepper

½ teaspoon ground cumin

½ teaspoon dried crushed red pepper

½ cup plain breadcrumbs

2 tablespoons canola oil

6 (4 by 4-inch) slices Monterey Jack cheese, cut in half crosswise

12 Waffle Buns (page 144; see Note), or 6 frozen Belgian waffles cut into quarters

Cilantro, Lime, and Green Chili Aioli (page 162)

2 ripe large avocados, pitted, peeled, and sliced

2 large Roma tomatoes, sliced

2 cups shredded iceberg lettuce

This is Taco Slider's hip and cool sibling. The one that everyone just heard about and has since garnered a reputation for being delicious and crazy good. Just because you don't eat meat doesn't mean you have to miss out on all the flavorful things the rest of us are eating. These sliders are made with healthy black bean patties, and are finished off with all of the usual taco toppings.

1. In a food processor, pulse half of the beans with the onion, garlic, cilantro, parsley, and egg until evenly combined. Pour into a large mixing bowl, and add the remaining half of the beans, the salt, black pepper, cumin, red pepper, and breadcrumbs. Stir until well combined. Form the mixture into 12 even patties, each about ½ inch thick.

2. Set a stovetop grill pan over medium-high heat. Brush the patties with oil and grill, in batches, for 4 to 6 minutes per side, until heated through and grill marks form. Place 2 pieces of cheese on top of each patty and cook on the grill until melted.

3. To assemble the sliders, spread aioli on all the waffles, and place a black bean patty on half the waffles. Top with a few slices of avocado, tomato, and lettuce and another waffle. Skewer with a long toothpick to hold in place. Serve immediately.

NOTE: For this recipe, make the Waffle Buns as directed but omit the scallions, bacon, and cheddar. These sliders are best with plain waffles!

spicy thai tofu sliders

YIELD: **12 sliders**

3 garlic cloves, minced

4 Thai chiles, chopped (see Note)

½ cup sugar

¼ cup rice wine vinegar

½ teaspoon kosher salt

1 tablespoon cornstarch

2 (14-ounce) packages extra-firm tofu, drained and rinsed

3 tablespoons canola or vegetable oil

12 Classic Potato Rolls (page 154) or store-bought slider buns or dinner rolls

Thai Peanut Sauce (page 172)

24 Thai basil leaves

1½ cups fresh bean sprouts

I've only just recently started experimenting with tofu. It's still very new to me, but I love how easily adaptable it is. There's nothing to be scared about when it comes to cooking with tofu. Sure, it comes packaged in a liquid, and okay, so maybe it looks and feels like a sponge, but it's actually really good. That spongy texture is exactly what you need in order for it to suck up all of those flavors being cooked with it. These sliders rely on some classic Thai ingredients in order to make the tofu shine.

1. Combine the garlic, chiles, sugar, ¾ cup water, the rice wine vinegar, and salt in a small saucepan and set over medium-high heat. Bring the mixture to a boil, decrease the heat to low, and simmer for about 5 minutes. In a small bowl, whisk together 2 more tablespoons of water with the cornstarch until it dissolves. Whisk into the sauce and cook until thickened, 1 to 2 minutes. Remove from heat and keep warm.

2. Place the tofu on a few paper towels set on a baking sheet. Cover with a few more paper towels and place a plate or platter on top with a few cans (from the pantry) to weigh it down. Let sit like this for about 15 minutes to fully drain any excess water. Cut into 1-inch slices.

3. Set a large skillet over high heat and add the oil. Once hot, carefully add the tofu (it might splatter a bit) in a single layer. Cook, a few slices at a time, until browned, 1 to 2 minutes per side. Transfer to the warm chile sauce, turning over to coat both sides. Repeat with the remaining tofu slices.

try these sliders with:

Braided Challah Buns (page 140)

Sweet Pineapple Hawaiian Rolls (page 152)

Classic Potato Rolls (page 154)

Cilantro, Lime, and Green Chili Aioli (page 162)

4. To assemble the sliders, split the rolls in half and spread each half with Thai peanut sauce. Cut a slice of tofu in half, stack both pieces on the bottom half of each roll, top with 2 basil leaves, a small handful of bean sprouts, and the top half of the rolls. Secure with a long toothpick to hold in place. Serve immediately.

NOTE: Keeping the seeds in the Thai chiles will make the sauce spicier; so if you'd like to tone down the heat somewhat, you can remove the seeds. Also, keep in mind that the chile sauce will be very spicy right when you make it. It'll become less spicy the longer it sits. Make it a few days in advance and just rewarm before using.

vegetable tempura sliders

Canola oil, for frying

1½ cups all-purpose flour, divided

1 tablespoon cornstarch

½ teaspoon kosher salt

1 large egg, lightly beaten

1½ cups cold seltzer water

24 or so (2-inch) vegetable pieces (such as slices of carrots, sweet potato, squash, bell pepper, onions, green beans, and/or broccoli; see Note)

12 Classic Potato Rolls (page 154) or store-bought slider buns or dinner rolls

Sriracha Aioli (page 162)

1 cup shredded carrots

1 medium cucumber, thinly sliced

6 green lettuce leaves, cut in half

½ cup soy sauce, for serving

I don't know about you, but whenever I eat sushi, I'm always hungry again two hours later. No matter how many rolls I eat, I never have enough. That's why before I order the sushi rolls, I start off with a few small non-sushi plates, like sesame chicken, dumplings, and vegetable tempura. Before you know it, I've spent all evening at the restaurant, just eating as much as humanly possible. It's an endless cycle that doesn't stop until someone forces me out of the place. These sliders are inspired by those endless trips to my favorite sushi house.

---

1. Set a large frying pan filled with about 2 inches of canola oil over medium-high heat. Heat until a deep-fry thermometer reaches 350°F.

2. In a large mixing bowl, combine 1 cup of the flour with the cornstarch, salt, egg, and seltzer water until combined. Be careful not to overmix. The batter will be lumpy, but that's okay.

3. Pour the remaining ½ cup flour into a shallow dish. Before coating the vegetables in the batter, pat them with a paper towel, making sure they're completely dry. Dust the vegetables in the flour and then dip into the batter. Set a wire rack over a baking sheet. Preheat the oven to 250°F.

4. Fry the vegetables, a few pieces at a time, until golden brown and crispy, 1 to 2 minutes per batch. Use chopsticks or tongs to flip over halfway through cooking. Drain and transfer to the wire rack. Keep warm in the oven while you fry the remaining vegetables.

5. To assemble the sliders, split the rolls in half and spread each half liberally with the aioli. Place a couple of pieces of fried vegetables, some of the shredded carrots, cucumber slices, and lettuce on each bottom half. Replace the top half of the rolls, and skewer with a long toothpick to hold in place. Serve immediately with soy sauce on the side for dipping.

NOTE: You can make it easy on yourself and use one type of vegetable for coating and frying in the tempura batter, or you can use a variety of veggies and surprise your guests.

try these sliders with:

Waffle Buns (page 144)

Crusty French Bread Rolls (page 150)

Sweet Pineapple Hawaiian Rolls (page 152)

Sweet and Spicy Honey Mustard (page 170)

afternoon snack sliders

YIELD: **12 sliders**

12 Black Pepper Buttermilk Biscuits (page 145) or store-bought biscuits

Spicy Pumpkin Chutney (page 165), or ½ cup store-bought apricot preserves

3 red Anjou pears, thinly sliced

¾ pound smoked Gouda, sliced

½ cup walnuts

¼ cup honey

try these sliders with:

Braided Challah Buns (page 140)

Rosemary Parmesan Focaccia Buns (page 148)

Sweet Pineapple Hawaiian Rolls (page 152)

Sweet and Spicy Honey Mustard (page 170)

Do you ever eat lunch and then a couple of hours later you're super hungry again? It's too early for dinner, but a quick snack is all you need. When that happens to me (which is often), I end up eating a few nuts, two slices of cheese, and a handful of crackers to get me through those midday hunger pains. This slider incorporates some of my favorite snacks into one tasty midday treat. It's easy to whip up, and great for dinner parties or casual gatherings with friends. Not a smoked Gouda fan? This slider would also be great with Brie or white cheddar cheese.

---

1. Split the biscuits in half and spread each bottom half with about a tablespoon of chutney (or preserves). Top with a few pear and cheese slices, a few walnuts, and a drizzle of honey.

2. Cover with the top of the biscuit and skewer with a toothpick to keep in place. Serve and enjoy immediately.

NOTE: The Black Pepper Buttermilk Biscuits (page 145) yield 9 biscuits, so you'll need to make a double batch for this recipe.

buns, rolls, and biscuits

Full disclosure: Freshly baked bread will ruin your life, forever. That's a guarantee. You'll never eat store-bought buns or rolls again. Watch as your guests instantly become impressed when they learn that you made your slider buns from scratch. You'll be a hero. Lucky for you, there are eleven different buns, rolls, and biscuits in this chapter to try. Everything Bagel Slider Buns (page 138), Sweet Pineapple Hawaiian Rolls (page 152), and Baked-Potato Buttermilk Biscuits (page 156) are just a few examples of what's in store. Each one is magnificent in its own right; each one is calling out your name. If you've never made bread from scratch, but have always wanted to, now is the time. You can do this—I believe in you. Here are a couple of things to remember to ensure your success.

YEAST

The yeast recipes in this chapter all require active dry yeast. There's no particular reason for that, other than I'm most comfortable with active dry yeast. If you're more of an instant-yeast type of baker, or that's all you have on hand, you can definitely use that instead. The rising time will be shorter, as you'll notice the dough doubles in size faster than when using active dry yeast. The best part about instant yeast is that you don't have to worry about activating the yeast— known as "proofing"—beforehand. It'll save you a bit of time and effort. Just mix the instant yeast right into the dry ingredients, according to the recipe directions.

RISING

Make the dough according to the recipe directions. Then let it rise in a warm, draft-free spot. I've found that the perfect temperature and environment for dough-rising are in a warm oven that is turned off. To prepare your oven for dough-rising, preheat it to 250°F for about ten minutes. Then shut it off and leave the door open for about ten minutes to cool slightly. Place your dough in the oven and close the door. Your dough should rise in one to two hours, depending on the recipe. I've also had great luck on top of the refrigerator (if your oven is occupied). Move those cereal boxes and make some room for your dough.

PROOFING ACTIVE DRY YEAST

To proof active dry yeast, you need at least ¼ cup of whatever liquid (such as water or milk) the recipe calls for. The temperature of the liquid is very important. It should be between 100°F and 110°F. It needs to be warm enough to wake up the yeast but not so hot that it kills the yeast before it has a chance to activate and foam up. You also need a teaspoon or so of sugar or honey to feed the yeast. Yeast is a living thing like you and me, and it needs food. Grab a bowl, fill it with the warm liquid, add the sugar or honey and let it dissolve, then sprinkle in the yeast. Place the bowl in a warm spot for ten minutes. If after ten minutes you notice that the yeast isn't foamy and creamy, toss it and start again.

KNEADING

It's important to knead your bread dough as much as possible before the initial rise. That develops the gluten and makes the bread light, airy, and chewy — all crucial characteristics of great-tasting bread. You can achieve this by hand, on a lightly floured work surface, kneading the dough with the palms of your hands and rotating the dough every so often, usually for eight to ten minutes. Alternatively, use a stand mixer fitted with the dough hook on high, usually for five to seven minutes.

5 TIPS FOR BECOMING A BETTER BREAD MAKER

1. Lose your fear. There is nothing scary about making bread. If anything, it's fun and relaxing. If you do mess up, have a laugh and start again from the beginning. Practice makes everything perfect.

2. Check the expiration dates on the flour and the yeast. How long have you had them sitting in your pantry? Both need to be as fresh as possible so that you can have the best bread possible.

3. Two rises are always better than one. You've just beaten the crap out of the dough, so it needs time to rest and recover. The first rise happens when you make the dough, and the other when you shape the buns/rolls/loaves, etc., right before baking.

4. Invest in a food thermometer. It's crucial for bread-making, and can also be used for everyday cooking. Most baked breads have an internal temperature of 190°F to 205°F.

5. All ovens are not the same. To make sure you don't burn your bread, or worse, undercook it, check the internal temperature of the bread about ten minutes before it's supposed to be done.

FREEZING

Some of the recipes in this chapter make more than enough buns for the slider recipes themselves. In a few instances, you'll have extra buns lying around. You can thank me later. The great thing about all of these bread recipes is that they freeze really well. If you have leftovers, or want to plan ahead, just pop them into a resealable plastic freezer bag and freeze until ready to eat. They will keep in the freezer for up to three months. A quick rewarming in a preheated 350°F oven for ten to fifteen minutes is all it takes to have fresh-tasting homemade bread. You'll be on your way to assembling the perfect slider in no time.

TOP ROW: Everything Bagel Slider Buns (page 138), Braided Challah Buns (page 140), Whole Wheat English Muffins (page 142), Waffle Buns (page 144)

MIDDLE ROW: Pretzel Buns (page 146), Rosemary Parmesan Focaccia Buns (page 148), Crusty French Bread Rolls (page 150), Sweet Pineapple Hawaiian Rolls (page 152)

BOTTOM ROW: Classic Potato Rolls (page 154), Black Pepper Buttermilk Biscuits (page 145), Baked-Potato Buttermilk Biscuits (page 156)

everything bagel slider buns

1½ cups warm whole
milk (about 110°F)

½ cup (1 stick) unsalted butter, diced

4½ teaspoons (two ¼-ounce
packets) active dry yeast

4 to 5 cups all-purpose flour,
plus more for dusting

¼ cup plus 1 tablespoon sugar

2 teaspoons table salt

2 egg yolks, whisked with
a splash of water

2 tablespoons sesame seeds

2 tablespoons poppy seeds

2 tablespoons kosher salt

2 tablespoons granulated onion

2 tablespoons granulated garlic

It's really true what they say about New York City bagels. They're out of this world. I could try and put into words just how delicious they are, but I wouldn't do them justice. I remember my very first trip to New York, where I proceeded to have an "everything bagel" every morning for a week straight. I came home and immediately devised a plan to make everything bagel slider buns because it seemed like the right thing to do. Now my slider buns taste just like everything bagels, but without any of the hard work. You can swap out the toppings of this recipe for other flavors to instantly transform these buns without much effort. Sprinkle just with sesame seeds for that authentic slider bun, or—my personal favorite—top with shredded cheddar and pickled jalapeño slices before baking for a cheesy kick.

1. Combine the milk and butter in a small pan and place over low heat. Cook until the butter has melted. Remove from the heat and let cool slightly to about 105°F to 115°F. Stir in the yeast. Let rest in a warm spot until dissolved, about 10 minutes.

2. In a large mixing bowl, whisk together 4 cups of the flour, the sugar, and table salt until combined. Pour in the yeast mixture and stir with a wooden spoon until the dough comes together. Add as much of the remaining cup of flour as needed, until the dough pulls away from the sides of the bowl. With a stand mixer fitted with the dough hook, knead on high for 4 to 5 minutes, or until smooth and somewhat elastic. (Alternatively, knead by hand for 8 to 10 minutes.) Transfer the dough to a lightly floured work surface and continue to knead, by hand, until soft and completely smooth and elastic, another 3 to 5 minutes. Oil a clean mixing bowl. Shape the dough into a ball and place in the bowl, turning over to coat both sides. Cover loosely with plastic wrap and a damp kitchen towel. Let rest in a warm spot until doubled in size, about 1½ hours.

3. Line 2 baking sheets with parchment paper. Transfer the dough to a lightly floured work surface, and divide into 24 even pieces. Roll each dough piece into a tight ball, between your palms or on the work surface. Place the balls on the prepared baking sheets, spacing them out evenly to allow room for spreading during baking. Cover loosely with plastic wrap and a damp kitchen towel. Let rest in a warm spot until doubled in size, about 30 minutes.

4. Preheat the oven to 375°F. Brush the buns with the egg wash and sprinkle each liberally with sesame seeds, poppy seeds, kosher salt, and granulated onion and garlic. Bake for 14 to 16 minutes, or until golden brown and shiny on top. Transfer the buns to a wire rack and let cool completely. Can be stored in an airtight container or plastic bag at room temperature for up to 1 week.

braided challah buns

YIELD: **about 15 mini buns**

4½ teaspoons (two ¼-ounce packets) active dry yeast

1 cup warm water (about 110°F)

¼ cup sugar, divided

3½ to 4 cups all-purpose flour

1¼ teaspoons salt

¼ cup vegetable oil, plus more for oiling bowl

4 large egg yolks

1 large egg, lightly beaten, for egg wash

2 tablespoons sesame seeds

Braiding challah can be a bit difficult, and it's even more strenuous when mini buns are involved. I spent many a night looking up online videos on how to perfect a challah braid before I started making these buns. It takes some getting used to, but nothing a little practice and patience can't solve. In the end, if all else fails, just roll this dough into balls and call it a day.

1. In a small bowl, combine the yeast, warm water, and 2 tablespoons of the sugar. Stir the mixture and let rest in a warm spot until foamy, about 10 minutes. If the yeast doesn't foam up, discard it and start over.

2. In a large bowl, combine 3 cups of the flour, the salt, the remaining 2 tablespoons sugar, ¼ cup oil, the egg yolks, and yeast mixture. Stir with a wooden spoon until the dough comes together in a rough ball. Add as much of the remaining flour as needed, little by little, until the dough forms a soft and somewhat sticky dough. Alternatively, you can mix and knead the dough in a stand mixer fitted with the dough hook.

3. Dump the dough onto a lightly floured work surface, and knead for 5 to 7 minutes, working in more flour as needed, until it forms a soft and smooth dough.

4. Oil a large bowl. Knead the dough into a ball and place it in the bowl. Turn over to coat both sides and cover loosely with plastic wrap and a damp kitchen towel. Allow to rest in a warm spot until doubled in size, about 1 hour. Punch the dough down, and let rest, covered, for another 45 minutes.

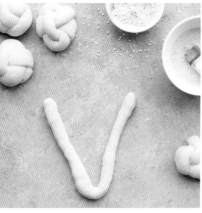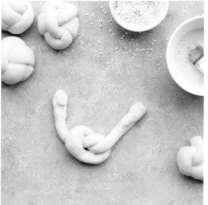

5. Transfer the dough onto a lightly floured work surface. Knead a few times and cut into 15 even pieces. Cover loosely with a damp towel to prevent drying. Line 2 baking sheets with parchment paper. Roll one dough piece into a 9-inch-long rope, and then tie the rope into a knot in the center. Make another knot right onto the first knot in the center and tuck the ends underneath. Place the braided bun on the prepared baking sheet. Repeat until all the dough pieces are braided. Preheat the oven to 350°F. Cover with plastic wrap and let rest for about 10 minutes while the oven heats up.

6. Brush each bun with the egg wash and sprinkle with sesame seeds. Bake for 25 to 30 minutes, or until golden brown. Remove from the oven and let cool for about 30 minutes. Will keep at room temperature in an airtight container for up to 5 days.

whole wheat english muffins

YIELD: **18 mini muffins**

2¼ teaspoons (¼-ounce packet) active dry yeast

⅓ cup warm water (about 110°F)

2 teaspoons honey

5 tablespoons unsalted butter, divided

½ cup plain Greek yogurt

½ cup warm whole milk (about 110°F)

1 teaspoon salt

1 cup whole wheat flour

1½ cups all-purpose flour

½ teaspoon baking soda

½ to ¾ cup yellow cornmeal

When I go out to a restaurant for breakfast or brunch, I always look forward to the toast more than the meal itself. I'll order my dish, and the server will ask me what kind of toast I'd like. I always ask what kind they have available, even though I know they pretty much have the usual suspects. The server begins to rattle off the list of breads: white, wheat, rye, sourdough . . . and I begin to contemplate each one, and just when I'm about to say whole wheat, the server mentions English muffin. My brain screeches to a halt and I know there's no debate. "English muffin" will forever and always be my answer. These are made into mini muffins so that they're the perfect size for our sliders!

---

1. In a small bowl, gently stir the yeast, warm water, and honey. Let rest in a warm spot until foamy, about 10 minutes. If the yeast doesn't foam up, discard it and start over.

2. Melt 2 tablespoons of the butter. In a large mixing bowl, whisk together the melted butter, the yogurt, milk, salt, and the yeast mixture. Add the flours and baking soda and mix thoroughly until well combined. Loosely cover bowl with plastic wrap and a damp kitchen towel and let rest in a warm spot until doubled in size, about 1½ hours.

3. Preheat the oven to 350°F. Lightly dust a baking sheet with cornmeal, and set aside.

4. Transfer the dough to a lightly floured work surface and knead a few times. Cut into 18 even pieces. Working with one dough piece at a time, roll gently on the work surface to shape into a smooth, round ball. Place the ball on the prepared baking sheet, and lightly flatten with the palm of your hand. Roll and flatten the rest of the dough pieces. Cover loosely with plastic wrap and let rest until doubled in size, about 1 hour.

5. Place a large cast-iron skillet or griddle over medium heat and add 1 tablespoon of the butter. Once melted, transfer the muffins to the skillet, a few at a time. Decrease the heat to low and cook until the bottoms are golden brown, 3 to 5 minutes. Flip the muffins over and cook for another 2 to 4 minutes to brown the opposite side. Return the muffins to the baking sheet and repeat with the remaining dough until all of the muffins are cooked, adding more butter as needed.

6. Bake the muffins until puffy and cooked through, 3 to 6 minutes. Let cool before splitting with a fork and using. The muffins can be stored at room temperature in an airtight container for up to 2 weeks! Just split with a fork and toast when ready to eat.

waffle buns

YIELD: **12 buns**
(2 triangles create 1 "bun")

2 large eggs, separated

2 cups all-purpose flour

2 tablespoons cornstarch

1 tablespoon baking powder

½ teaspoon cayenne pepper

½ teaspoon salt

2 tablespoons sugar

½ cup vegetable or canola oil

2 cups buttermilk

4 scallions, thinly sliced

¾ cup grated cheddar cheese

I learned that the secret to making the best waffles is adding cornstarch to the dry ingredients. It helps keep them crispy on the outside and soft and chewy on the inside. Just the way you want waffles to be. Feel free to use this secret for all of your waffle-making adventures. The green onion and cheddar cheese take these waffles to the next level of deliciousness and make them the perfect savory vehicle for sliders. This recipe makes super-extra-thick waffles, so make sure you use a deep-cavity Belgian waffle maker.

1. In a large clean mixing bowl, with a mixer, beat the egg whites on high until stiff peaks form, 6 to 8 minutes. Set aside.

2. In a large bowl, whisk together the flour, cornstarch, baking powder, cayenne, salt, and sugar. Set aside.

3. Stir together the egg yolks, oil, and buttermilk in a separate bowl. Pour the egg yolk mixture into the dry ingredients and fold with a rubber spatula until just combined. Fold in the beaten egg whites, being careful not to overmix. Lastly, stir in the scallions and cheddar cheese.

4. Preheat a Belgian waffle iron. Set a wire rack over a baking sheet. Scoop about ¼ cup of the batter, depending on the size of your waffle iron, into the center. Cook according to the manufacturer's directions. Waffles should be golden brown and crispy on the outside. Transfer to the wire rack to cool, and continue until all the batter is used. Cut the waffles into triangles. Leftovers can be stored in the refrigerator in an airtight container for up to 3 days or in the freezer for about 3 weeks. Rewarm in a preheated 250°F oven for about 5 minutes or in a toaster.

black pepper buttermilk biscuits

YIELD: **9 biscuits**

2 cups all-purpose flour

1 tablespoon baking powder

¼ teaspoon baking soda

1 teaspoon salt

6 tablespoons very cold unsalted butter, diced, plus 2 tablespoons, melted

1 cup buttermilk

2 tablespoons coarsely ground black pepper

Biscuits can be really difficult to make, but once you get the hang of it, they can be super easy. Ditch the rolling pin, food processor, and stand mixer for this recipe; do it all by hand, the old-fashioned way. Work quickly though, so that the bits of butter throughout the dough remain cold. If you follow those rules, you'll have perfect flaky biscuits each and every time. These are also great without the black pepper, for delicious plain biscuits.

1. Preheat the oven to 425°F. Line a baking sheet with parchment paper, and set aside.

2. In a large mixing bowl, combine the flour, baking powder, baking soda, and salt. Add the cold butter and cut in using 2 knives, a pastry blender, potato masher, or your hands, until the dough resembles coarse crumbs the size of peas.

3. Add the buttermilk and stir with a wooden spoon until the dough just comes together. It'll be a sticky dough. Transfer to a well-floured work surface and knead a few times to smooth it out. Fold the dough onto itself about 4 times, turning clockwise after each fold. Pat the dough with your hands until it's about ¾ inch thick.

4. Use a 2-inch round cookie or biscuit cutter to cut into rounds. Place the biscuits on the prepared baking sheet just barely touching each other.

5. Brush the tops with the melted butter, and sprinkle with the pepper. Bake until golden brown, 10 to 12 minutes. Let cool before serving. Store any leftovers in an airtight container in the refrigerator for up to 4 days.

pretzel buns

YIELD: **16 small buns**

DOUGH

1½ cups warm water (about 110°F)

2¼ (¼-ounce packet) active dry yeast

1 tablespoon malt barley
syrup or dark brown sugar

4½ cups all-purpose flour, divided

2 teaspoons salt

4 tablespoons unsalted butter,
melted and cooled

BOILING SOLUTION

¼ cup baking soda

2 tablespoons malt barley
syrup (optional)

TOPPING

1 large egg

2 to 4 tablespoons pretzel salt

One rule of thumb when it comes to bread-making: homemade pretzel buns are ALWAYS worth all of the time and effort. You might convince yourself that they aren't and talk yourself out of making them, but don't. Go ahead and make these pretzels buns—you deserve it. Your friends and family deserve it. Make sure you have mustard on hand, though, because you're going to want to eat one right out of the oven with mustard. I guarantee it. Malt barley syrup is what gives pretzels that authentic taste and dark crusty exterior. You can find it at most specialty food stores or online, along with the pretzel salt.

---

1. In the bowl of a stand mixer fitted with the paddle attachment, combine the warm water, yeast, and malt barley syrup (or sugar), and let rest in a warm spot until foamy, about 10 minutes. If the yeast doesn't foam up, discard it and start over.

2. Add 3 cups of flour, the salt, and butter to the yeast mixture. Mix until well combined, about 3 minutes. Switch to the dough hook and beat on medium, adding as much of the remaining 1½ cups of flour as needed, until the dough pulls away from the sides. Knead on high until smooth and elastic, 7 to 10 minutes. Transfer the dough to a lightly floured work surface and knead a few times by hand to form a ball. Oil a large bowl and place the dough in the bowl, turning over to coat both sides. Cover with plastic wrap and a damp kitchen towel and let rest in a warm spot until doubled in size, about 1½ hours.

3. Line a baking sheet with parchment paper. Punch the dough down and transfer to a work surface. Divide into 16 even pieces. Cover with a damp kitchen towel, to prevent drying. Working with one dough piece at a time, using the palm of your hand, roll into a tight ball on the work surface. Place on the prepared baking sheet and roll the rest of the dough pieces. Cover loosely with plastic wrap and let rest in a warm spot until doubled in size, about 30 minutes.

4. Preheat the oven to 425°F. Fill a large pot halfway with water and bring to a boil. Add the baking soda and malt barley syrup, if using. Return to a simmer. Carefully drop 2 or 3 dough balls into the simmering water. Boil for about 30 seconds, flip, and continue to boil for another 30 seconds on the second side. Remove from the water, using a slotted spoon, and return to the baking sheet. Boil the rest of the dough balls.

5. Whisk the egg with a splash of water and brush the tops of the buns. Using a sharp knife or a razor blade, cut an X on the top of each bun. Sprinkle with pretzel salt and bake for 15 to 20 minutes, until golden brown on top. Remove from the oven and let cool completely on a wire rack before serving. Leftovers can be stored in an airtight container at room temperature for up to 4 days.

rosemary parmesan focaccia buns

YIELD: **16 small buns**

1 cup warm water (about 110°F)

2¼ teaspoons (¼-ounce packet) active dry yeast

2 teaspoons honey

2½ cups all-purpose flour

2 teaspoons salt

¼ cup plus 2 tablespoons olive oil for greasing baking sheet

2 tablespoons chopped fresh rosemary

¼ cup grated Parmesan cheese

I have this crazy dream where I sleep on a pillow made of fluffy soft focaccia bread. It's more like a fantasy that I hope one day comes to life, and if my focaccia pillow is topped with rosemary and Parmesan like this one is, I wouldn't be mad. In fact, I'd be the happiest person on the planet. This is one of those recipes that are very versatile. Feel free to swap out the rosemary and Parmesan for other toppings, like sliced tomato, garlic, different herbs, olives, or even goat cheese.

---

1. In a small bowl, gently stir the warm water, yeast, and honey. Let rest in a warm spot until foamy, about 10 minutes. If the yeast doesn't foam up, discard it and start over.

2. In the bowl of a stand mixer fitted with the paddle attachment, combine the flour, salt, ¼ cup of the olive oil, and yeast mixture until the dough begins to come together. Switch to the dough hook. Knead the dough on high for 5 to 7 minutes, until it becomes soft and somewhat elastic.

3. Transfer the dough to a well-floured work surface and knead a few times by hand. Oil a bowl well. Shape the dough into a ball and place in the bowl, turning over to coat both sides. Cover loosely with plastic wrap and a damp kitchen towel. Let rest in a warm spot until doubled in size, about 1 hour

4. Line a baking sheet with parchment paper and drizzle with the remaining 2 tablespoons olive oil. Transfer the dough to the prepared baking sheet and stretch out with your hands to fully cover the baking sheet with dough. Using your fingers, make indentations all across the top. Cover with plastic wrap and a damp kitchen towel and let rest in a warm spot for another hour.

5. Preheat the oven to 400°F. Sprinkle the bread evenly over the top with the rosemary and Parmesan. Bake the focaccia until golden brown on top, 20 to 25 minutes. Remove from the oven and let cool down before cutting. Cut into 16 squares and use immediately. Any leftovers can be stored in an airtight container at room temperature for up to 3 days.

crusty french bread rolls

YIELD: **24 small rolls**

2¼ teaspoons (¼-ounce packet) active dry yeast

2¼ cups warm water (about 110°F)

1 tablespoon sugar

5 cups all-purpose flour, divided

2 teaspoons salt

1 large egg

1 tablespoon whole milk

After a trip to the grocery store, you can often find me driving home with a baguette in my hand, just eating it while I drive, as if it were a normal everyday occurrence. That's how much I love a crusty French bread. If you weren't a believer before, these rolls will definitely convert you. You might even eat them in the car while driving. Who am I to judge?

1. In the bowl of a stand mixer fitted with the paddle attachment, dissolve the yeast in the warm water. Stir in the sugar and let rest in a warm spot until foamy and doubled in size, about 45 minutes. If the yeast doesn't foam up, discard it and start over.

2. Stir in 3 cups of flour and the salt and beat on low until smooth, 5 to 7 minutes. Switch to the dough hook and beat on medium, adding as much of the remaining 2 cups of flour as needed, until the dough comes together and pulls away from the sides of the bowl.

3. Transfer the dough to a lightly floured work surface and knead by hand until smooth and elastic, about 5 minutes. Oil a bowl. Transfer the dough to the bowl, turn over to coat both sides, and cover loosely with plastic wrap and a damp kitchen towel. Let rest in a warm spot until doubled in size, about 1½ hours.

4. Punch the dough down and transfer to a lightly floured work surface. Divide into 24 even pieces and cover with a damp kitchen towel, to prevent drying. Line 2 baking sheets with parchment paper. Working with one piece at a time, roll the dough between your hands on the work surface, until it forms a tight ball. Place on a prepared sheet, and roll the rest of the dough pieces, evenly spacing them out as you place on the baking sheets.

5. Cover the baking sheets loosely with plastic wrap and let rest in a warm spot until doubled in size, about 30 minutes. Preheat the oven to 400°F.

6. Whisk the egg and milk together and brush on top of the rolls. Using a sharp knife or razor blade, cut a 1-inch slit down the center of each roll. Bake for 20 to 25 minutes, or until golden brown (see Tip). Transfer the rolls to a wire rack and let cool completely before serving. Store any leftovers in an airtight container at room temperature for up to 4 days.

NOTE: For extra-crusty rolls, fill a spray bottle with water and spray the bottom of the oven a few times during the baking process to create steam.

sweet pineapple hawaiian rolls

⅓ cup warm whole milk (about 110°F)

2¼ teaspoons (¼-ounce packet) active dry yeast

½ cup plus 1 tablespoon packed light brown sugar, divided

¼ cup vegetable oil

¼ cup unsalted butter, melted and cooled

3 large eggs

1 (8-ounce) can crushed pineapple, with juice

4 to 5 cups all-purpose flour

1 teaspoon salt

When I was a kid, we used to eat grocery-store fried chicken once or twice a month. You know, that crispy ready-to-go fried chicken from the local supermarket. It was a treat that I not-so-secretly loved. If you bought an eight-piece meal, you'd get a package of sweet Hawaiian rolls. So I'd beg my mom to get the meal, and I'd eat all of the sweet rolls myself, because fried chicken and sweet Hawaiian rolls are long-lost lovers.

1. In the bowl of a stand mixer fitted with the paddle attachment, combine the milk, yeast, and 1 tablespoon of the brown sugar. Let rest in a warm spot until foamy, about 10 minutes. If the yeast doesn't foam up, discard it and start over.

2. Add the remaining ½ cup sugar, the oil, butter, 2 eggs, pineapple, 4 cups of the flour, and the salt to the milk and yeast mixture. Beat on low for a minute or two to combine. Switch to the dough hook and beat on medium, adding as much of the remaining flour as needed, until the dough forms a shaggy and somewhat soft dough. Knead on high for 7 to 10 minutes, until smooth and elastic. Dough will be very sticky. Transfer to a lightly floured work surface and knead a few times to form a ball. Lightly oil a bowl. Place dough in the bowl, turning over to coat both sides, and cover loosely with plastic wrap and a damp kitchen towel. Let rest in a warm spot until doubled in size, about 1½ hours.

3. Punch the dough down and transfer to a work surface. Divide into 24 even pieces. Cover with a damp kitchen towel, to prevent drying. Line a baking sheet with parchment paper. Working with one dough piece at a time, roll into a tight ball. Arrange on the prepared baking sheet, and roll the rest of the dough pieces, spacing them evenly as you place on the baking sheets. Cover loosely with plastic wrap and let rest in a warm spot until doubled in size, about 40 minutes. Preheat the oven to 375°F.

4. Whisk the remaining egg with a splash of water, brushing the tops of the rolls with the egg wash. Bake for 20 to 25 minutes, until golden brown. Remove from the oven and let cool completely on a wire rack before serving. Store any leftovers in an airtight container at room temperature for up to 4 days.

classic potato rolls

1 medium to large baking
potato, rinsed and dried

4¼ cups all-purpose flour, divided

2¼ teaspoons (¼-ounce
packet) active dry yeast

3 large eggs, at room temperature

⅓ cup sugar

6 tablespoons butter,
melted and cooled

¾ cup warm water (about 110°F)

Two bread recipes with potatoes in them—I'm out of my mind,
but at the same time, I might just be a genius. No one really
knows. These soft rolls are great for any number of sliders
because their subtle flavor adapts well to so many recipes.

1. Cook the potato in the microwave or in boiling water until
fork-tender. Let cool completely, then peel, and mash using a
fork until somewhat smooth.

2. In the bowl of a stand mixer fitted with the paddle
attachment, combine 2 cups of flour with the yeast.

3. In a separate bowl, whisk together 2 eggs, the sugar, butter,
mashed potato, and warm water. Add to the flour and yeast
mixture.

4. Mix on low for about 25 seconds, then raise the speed to
high and continue to beat for another 3 minutes. Switch to
the dough hook and knead on medium, adding as much of the
remaining flour as needed, until the dough pulls away from the
sides of the bowl, about 7 minutes.

5. Oil a clean bowl well. Transfer the dough to the bowl and
cover with plastic wrap. Refrigerate for about 2 hours and up
to 24 hours.

6. Punch the dough down lightly and transfer to a lightly
floured work surface. Knead 4 or 5 times by hand, cover with a
damp kitchen towel, and let rest for about 15 minutes.

7. Line 2 baking sheets with parchment paper. Divide the dough into 24 even pieces and cover with a towel once again. Working with one piece at a time, roll between your hands on the work surface to shape into a tight ball. Place on a baking sheet, about 2 inches apart. Repeat with the remaining pieces, spacing them out evenly on the baking sheets.

8. Cover and let rest in a warm spot until doubled in size, about 30 minutes. Meanwhile, preheat the oven to 375°F. Whisk the remaining egg with a splash of water and brush the tops of the rolls with it. Bake until golden brown, 16 to 20 minutes. Let cool down on a wire rack before serving. Leftovers can be stored in an airtight container at room temperature for up to 4 days.

baked-potato buttermilk biscuits

YIELD: **9 biscuits**

1 medium baking potato, rinsed and dried

2 cups all-purpose flour

1 tablespoon baking powder

¼ teaspoon baking soda

1 teaspoon salt

½ teaspoon coarsely ground black pepper

6 tablespoons very cold unsalted butter, diced, plus 2 tablespoons, melted

¼ cup shredded white cheddar cheese

2 tablespoons chopped chives

1 cup buttermilk

I have a love of potatoes that is unlike any other love. I grew up eating them often as a kid—almost every day—so now I'm always looking for new ways to incorporate this versatile vegetable into my everyday life. There's just something so special about biscuits loaded with shredded potatoes, cheddar cheese, and chives. I can't put it into words, but I feel like I don't have to because you get it. It's the baked potato you never knew you wanted . . . in biscuit form.

1. Preheat the oven to 425°F. Line a baking sheet with parchment paper, and set aside.

2. Cook the potato in a microwave, an oven, or in boiling water until almost fork-tender (see Note). Let cool completely. Using a paring knife, peel the potato, and then shred with a box grater.

3. In a large mixing bowl, combine the flour, baking powder, baking soda, salt, and pepper. Add the cold butter and cut in using 2 knives, a pastry blender, potato masher, or your hands, until the dough resembles coarse crumbs the size of peas. Fold in the cheese, chives, and shredded potato.

4. Add the buttermilk and stir with a wooden spoon until the dough just comes together. It'll be sticky, but don't panic. Transfer to a well-floured work surface and knead a few times to smooth it out. Fold the dough onto itself about 4 times, turning clockwise after each fold. Pat the dough with your hands until it's about ¾ inch thick.

5. Use a 2-inch round cookie or biscuit cutter to cut into rounds. Place the biscuits on the prepared baking pan just barely touching each other.

6. Brush the biscuits with the melted butter, and bake until golden brown, 10 to 12 minutes. Let cool before serving. Store any leftovers in an airtight container in the refrigerator for up to 4 days.

NOTE: If you cook the potato all the way, it'll be really difficult to peel and grate later on, so make sure to cook it just a bit shy of almost done. I use the microwave to make it easy and fast.

sauces, spreads, and condiments

Do you have a favorite sauce for dipping, spreading, and drenching some, if not most, of your favorite dishes? I do; in fact I have quite a handful of sauces I can't live without. In this chapter, I'll share them all with you. I've learned the hard way that no slider is complete without some type of condiment to bring all the flavors together. It's a key element in a lot of recipes, not just sliders. Ketchup, yellow mustard, and mayo are great as a starting point, but they're also a bit boring and predictable. Let's venture out into something more intriguing and impressive; you'll be so glad you did. These twelve homemade sauces, spreads, and condiments are here to save the day. Their main task is to take your sliders from ordinary to extraordinary.

I know that you don't always have the time to make every component of a dish from scratch. We all have lives with not enough hours in the day. So if you don't have time, each of these sauces can be made in advance and stored in the refrigerator until ready to use, or can be substituted with a corresponding store-bought counterpart. My easy-to-make go-to Barbecue Sauce (page 164) is perfect for all of your grilling needs, and is used many times in the book. Sweet and Spicy Strawberry-Rhubarb Tomato Ketchup (page 171) is a childhood classic with a grown-up twist. And the Home-made Aioli (page 160) can be adapted three different ways. As you'll find, there's something for everyone.

homemade aioli, three ways

YIELD: about 1 cup

3 garlic cloves, smashed and peeled

1 large egg, (see Note, page 161)

1 tablespoon fresh lemon juice

1 tablespoon Dijon mustard

1 cup canola oil

½ teaspoon kosher salt

¼ teaspoon coarsely ground black pepper

Aioli is the type of sauce you want to invite to every party. Use it as a dip for crispy fries, a sauce for topping those boring vegetables with, or as a spread for sandwiches—and of course, on sliders. Start with a great base of just a handful of ingredients—which, chances are, you probably already have lying around—and then add in whatever flavors you like. Here are three different ways to liven up your homemade aioli!

1. Place the garlic, egg, lemon juice, and mustard in a blender. Blend until just combined. With the machine running on high, slowly stream in the oil and blend until incorporated and the mixture has thickened. Season with salt and pepper and pulse once more.

2. Transfer to a bowl or jar and chill, covered tightly, until ready to use. Will keep in refrigerator for up to 2 weeks.

NOTE: If the aioli becomes too thick, add a few drops of water to thin it out.

continued on page 162

CLOCKWISE, FROM TOP LEFT:
Thai Peanut Sauce (page 172), Spicy Pumpkin Chutney (page 165), Arugula Pumpkin Seed Pesto (page 167), Hummus (page 163), Red Wine Marinara (page 169), Barbecue Sauce (page 164), Cajun Rémoulade (page 166) Sweet and Spicy Honey Mustard (page 170), Chimichurri (page 168), Sweet and Spicy Strawberry-Rhubarb Tomato Ketchup (page 171), Cilantro, Lime, and Green Chili Aioli (page 162), Roasted Garlic Aioli (page 162), Sriracha Aioli (page 162), Buttermilk Ranch Dressing (page 170)

homemade aioli, three ways

continued

roasted garlic aioli

10 garlic cloves, smashed and peeled

1 tablespoon olive oil

½ teaspoon kosher salt

¼ teaspoon coarsely
ground black pepper

1. Preheat the oven to 400°F.

2. Place the garlic cloves on a couple of sheets of aluminum foil. Drizzle with the olive oil, salt, and pepper and toss to evenly combine. Wrap the foil around the garlic into a tight package and roast in the oven until tender and caramelized, 20 to 25 minutes. Remove from oven and let cool.

3. Add the roasted garlic to the aioli at the end of step 1 in the main recipe, and blend until combined.

sriracha aioli

1 to 2 tablespoons Sriracha
(depending on how hot you like it)

1. Add the Sriracha to the aioli at the end of step 1 in the main recipe, and blend until combined.

cilantro, lime, and green chili aioli

2 teaspoons finely grated lime zest

1 tablespoon fresh lime juice

1 (4-ounce) can green chiles, drained

¼ cup fresh cilantro, roughly chopped

1. Add the lime zest, lime juice, green chiles, and cilantro to the aioli at the end of step 1 in the main recipe, and blend until combined.

NOTE: If you're concerned about using raw eggs, you can substitute the egg in this recipe with a pasteurized whole egg.

hummus

YIELD: **about 1½ cups**

1 (15.5-ounce) can garbanzo
beans, drained and rinsed

3 tablespoons tahini (see Note)

Finely grated zest and juice
from 1 medium lemon

2 tablespoons extra-virgin olive oil

1 teaspoon kosher salt

½ teaspoon coarsely
ground black pepper

1 large garlic clove, peeled

½ teaspoon ground cumin

½ teaspoon dried oregano

¼ teaspoon cayenne
pepper or chili powder

There is a special place in my heart for hummus, along with doughnuts and potatoes. Hummus is right up there as one of my all-time favorite snacks. It's so tempting to pick up a container at the grocery store—even I've succumbed to that sad fate on several occasions—but when you really think about it, it's so much easier to make at home. Just let the food processor do all the work for you. Those days of going down the refrigerated foods aisle in the middle of the night for a container of hummus are long gone.

1. Place all of the ingredients in a food processor with 2 tablespoons water and blend until smooth. Stop and scrape the sides and bottom of the bowl, as needed. If the hummus is too thick, add a bit more water to thin it out until the desired consistency is reached. I prefer my hummus on the thicker side.

2. Transfer to an airtight container and store in the refrigerator until ready to use. Can be kept in the fridge for up to 4 days.

NOTE: Tahini is a ground sesame seed paste that's a key ingredient in hummus. You can find it in most major grocery stores in the Middle Eastern foods aisle.

barbecue sauce

YIELD: **about 1½ cups**

1 tablespoon vegetable or canola oil

1 small yellow onion, diced

2 garlic cloves, minced

1 tablespoon tomato paste

1 (8-ounce) can tomato sauce (no salt added)

¼ cup bourbon (optional)

2 tablespoons packed light brown sugar

2 tablespoons apple cider vinegar

2 tablespoons molasses

1 tablespoon Worcestershire sauce

2 teaspoons Dijon mustard

1 teaspoon liquid smoke (see Note)

1 teaspoon kosher salt

½ teaspoon coarsely ground black pepper

½ teaspoon granulated onion

½ teaspoon granulated garlic

½ teaspoon ground cumin

¼ teaspoon dried crushed red pepper

Couple dashes hot sauce

Something about making my own barbecue sauce at home scared me for the longest time. In my mind I always pictured a never-ending list of ingredients and hours and hours of cooking time. I didn't have the time or patience, until one day I was in need of barbecue sauce but was too lazy to go to the store. We've all been there. This is now my go-to recipe for barbecue sauce at home, which just happens to be short and to the point. That gives me more time to drench everything in this addicting sauce. It's a win-win.

1. Place the oil in a medium saucepan over medium-high heat. Once hot, add the onion and garlic, sautéing until translucent and just beginning to caramelize, about 5 minutes.

2. Stir in the tomato paste, tomato sauce, bourbon if using, brown sugar, vinegar, molasses, Worcestershire sauce, Dijon mustard, liquid smoke, salt, black pepper, granulated onion, granulated garlic, cumin, red pepper, and hot sauce, and bring to a boil. Lower the heat and simmer, stirring occasionally, until thickened and reduced by a third, about 10 minutes. If the sauce becomes too thick, add a splash of water to thin it out. Let cool slightly before transferring to a glass jar with a tight-fitting lid. Store in the fridge until ready to use. Can be made up to 2 weeks in advance. Use at room temperature.

NOTE: Liquid smoke is an optional ingredient, but it does add that smoky mesquite flavor to the BBQ sauce that makes it so tasty and authentic. If you can't find liquid smoke at the grocery store, try looking online!

spicy pumpkin chutney

YIELD: **about 2 cups**

2 tablespoons canola oil

1 small yellow onion, diced

5 garlic cloves, chopped

2 teaspoons grated fresh gingerroot

3 small red chiles, chopped

2 teaspoons cayenne pepper

½ teaspoon ground coriander

½ teaspoon curry powder

½ teaspoon ground cumin

1 (16-ounce) can pumpkin purée

⅓ cup tomato paste

2 tablespoons fresh lemon juice

1 teaspoon salt

1 teaspoon mustard seeds, toasted and crushed (see Note)

⅓ cup white vinegar

2 tablespoons sugar

¼ cup apricot preserves

2 tablespoons chopped fresh cilantro

There's a local Indian restaurant I frequent far too often, which serves spicy pumpkin chutney. Sure, their food is delicious, but the real reason they can't get rid of me is this chutney in particular. After I'm done devouring the rice crackers that come with it, I start to drench everything else in the chutney as well. By my fourth bowl of chutney, they have to ask me to leave. I've since started making it at home for myself, which has become a real problem.

1. Place the oil in a large saucepan over medium-high heat. Once hot, add the onion, garlic, ginger, chiles, cayenne, coriander, curry powder, and cumin. Cook until translucent and fragrant, 2 to 3 minutes. Stir in the pumpkin, tomato paste, lemon juice, salt, mustard seeds, vinegar, sugar, apricot preserves, and ½ cup of water. Decrease the heat to low and simmer for 25 to 30 minutes, stirring often so that the chutney doesn't burn. Add the cilantro and cook for another 10 minutes, continuously stirring.

2. Remove from the heat and let cool completely. Transfer to an airtight container and place in the fridge until ready to use. Can be kept for up to 5 days.

NOTE: Toast the mustard seeds in a dry skillet over low to medium heat, just for a few minutes. Make sure to toss around in the pan often so they don't burn. Transfer to a mortar and pestle and grind. You can also place them in a plastic food storage bag and smash them with the bottom of a skillet.

cajun rémoulade

¼ cup mayonnaise

¼ cup dill pickle relish, drained

3 tablespoons Creole or grainy mustard

2 tablespoons minced yellow onion

2 tablespoons minced celery

2 tablespoons minced red bell pepper

2 tablespoons chopped parsley

1 tablespoon ketchup

1 tablespoon fresh lemon juice

1 garlic clove, minced

Couple dashes of hot sauce

Pinch of kosher salt, plus more if desired

Few grinds of fresh black pepper, plus more if desired

New Orleans happens to be one of my favorite cities to visit. The people are friendly, the drinks are plentiful, and the food is on another level. I'd say I would move there, but hot and humid weather just isn't for me. On days when I'm missing the Big Easy, I find myself making this Cajun rémoulade. Did I mention it goes well with fried green tomatoes and shrimp? It does, my friends, it does.

1. For a smooth sauce, combine all of the ingredients in a food processor and process until finely chopped and well combined. Alternatively, for a more rustic sauce, combine everything in a bowl and stir until evenly incorporated.

2. Give the sauce a taste and adjust seasonings accordingly, adding more salt or pepper if needed. Transfer to an airtight container and store in the refrigerator until ready to use. Can be kept, chilled, for up to 3 days.

arugula pumpkin seed pesto

YIELD: **about 1 cup**

2 cups packed fresh baby arugula

2 small garlic cloves, peeled

2 tablespoons pumpkin seeds, toasted

¼ cup grated Parmesan cheese

1 teaspoon finely grated lemon zest

1 tablespoon fresh lemon juice

½ cup extra-virgin olive oil

Pinch of kosher salt

Few grinds of fresh black pepper

I didn't grow up eating pesto as a kid. I doubt I even knew what it was back then. As I got older and began cooking, I started making it for my family all of the time. It became something they requested several nights a week. I like to swap out traditional ingredients like basil and pine nuts for arugula and pumpkin seeds, for a more robust flavor.

---

1. Place the arugula, garlic, pumpkin seeds, Parmesan, and lemon zest and juice in a food processor and pulse a few times until roughly chopped. Use a rubber spatula to scrape down the sides and bottom of the bowl between pulses, to ensure that everything is evenly chopped.

2. With the machine running, slowly drizzle in the olive oil in a steady stream. Process for about 30 seconds. Season with salt and pepper and pulse once more. Give the pesto a taste and adjust the seasonings if needed. Transfer to an airtight container and store in the fridge until ready to use (see Note). Can be kept, chilled, for up to 4 days.

NOTE: I like to place a piece of plastic wrap directly on top of the pesto, so it's touching the surface, then seal the container tightly with the lid. This will ensure that your pesto stays vibrant and green in the fridge!

chimichurri

YIELD: **about 1½ cups**

2 cups packed fresh Italian
parsley leaves

½ cup packed fresh cilantro leaves

¼ cup fresh oregano leaves (see Note)

¼ cup red wine vinegar

½ teaspoon kosher salt,
plus more if desired

¼ teaspoon coarsely ground black
pepper, plus more if desired

¼ teaspoon to ½ teaspoon
dried crushed red pepper

1 cup extra-virgin olive oil

If I could drench a steak or a piece of chicken in chimichurri everyday, I'd be the happiest person on the planet. Sadly, it doesn't always work out that way. I do, however, make sure to have this sauce on hand at all times because you never know when you're going to need it. A perfectly grilled steak could just appear out of nowhere one day. We need to be prepared for anything. The sauce tastes even better as it sits in the fridge, so if you have the time to make this a day in advance, go for it. You'll be glad you did!

1. Chop the parsley, cilantro, and oregano on a cutting board, running your knife back and forth across the herbs, until they're finally chopped.

2. Transfer the herbs to a medium mixing bowl, and stir in the vinegar, ½ teaspoon salt, ¼ teaspoon black pepper, and the red pepper. Drizzle in the olive oil, in a slow steady stream, whisking continuously until well combined.

3. Transfer the sauce to an airtight container and refrigerate for at least 2 hours. Readjust the seasonings, adding more salt and pepper if needed, right before serving. Serve at room temperature. Can be stored in the refrigerator for up to 1 week.

NOTE: If you can't find fresh oregano at the grocery store, use 4 teaspoons of dried oregano instead. Remember, when using dried herbs, less is more!

red wine marinara

YIELD: **about 2 cups**

1 tablespoon olive oil

1 small yellow onion, chopped

2 medium garlic cloves, minced

1 tablespoon tomato paste

½ cup red wine (see Note)

1 (28-ounce) can crushed tomatoes

1 teaspoon kosher salt

½ teaspoon coarsely
ground black pepper

½ teaspoon dried oregano

¼ teaspoon dried crushed red pepper

2 tablespoons chopped
fresh Italian parsley

2 tablespoons chopped fresh basil

I feel like everyone needs to know how to make marinara sauce. It's one of those recipes that can save you from no-time-to-cook hunger. Whip up a few batches and keep them in the fridge for those weekdays when you're just too tired to cook something elaborate. Toss the sauce with cooked pasta and call it dinner. If the marinara sauce finds its way onto chicken Parmesan or as a dip for fried mozzarella, I won't be mad.

1. Heat the olive oil in a medium saucepan over medium-high heat. Once hot, add the onion and garlic and sauté until translucent and just beginning to brown, 5 to 10 minutes. Stir in the tomato paste and wine. Cook on high heat, scraping the bottom of the pan with a wooden spoon, until most of the wine evaporates, about 3 minutes.

2. Add the crushed tomatoes, salt, black pepper, oregano, red pepper, parsley, and basil. Stir to evenly combine and simmer on low until reduced slightly, about 25 minutes. Use warm. Leftovers can be transferred to an airtight container and kept in the fridge for up to 4 days.

NOTE: Use any full-bodied red wine you prefer. Chianti or Cabernet Sauvignon work really well in this recipe.

sweet and spicy honey mustard

YIELD: **about 1 cup**

¼ cup yellow mustard

¼ cup Dijon mustard

¼ cup mild-flavored honey

1 tablespoon rice wine vinegar

2 to 3 tablespoons hot
sauce (Sriracha is great)

½ to 1 teaspoon dried crushed red
pepper (depending on your taste)

I'm not ashamed to admit that I grew up eating chicken nuggets from a well-known fast-food restaurant. I also ate only the boot-shaped pieces, but that's a story for another time. The only way I'd eat those delicious nuggets was by dipping them into an obscene amount of hot mustard. It was the greatest treat ever.

1. Combine all of the ingredients in a medium bowl, whisking until completely smooth. Transfer to an airtight container and chill for about 4 hours before using. Can be stored in the fridge for up to 4 days.

buttermilk ranch dressing

YIELD: **1½ cups**

¾ cup buttermilk

¼ cup mayonnaise

¼ cup sour cream

3 tablespoons chopped
fresh Italian parsley

2 tablespoons chopped chives

1 tablespoon white wine vinegar

1 small garlic clove, minced

½ teaspoon salt

¼ teaspoon coarsely
ground black pepper

I enjoy my ranch like I enjoy my cocktails, cold and bursting with flavor. I won't say that I eat ranch all by itself by the spoonful, but I also won't say that I *couldn't* eat it by itself. I'll load it on top of everything from salads and sandwiches, to chicken, vegetables, and even pizza. Yes, especially pizza.

1. Combine all of the ingredients in a medium bowl, whisking until smooth. Transfer to an airtight container or jar with a tight-fitting lid and chill for at least 1 hour. The dressing can be kept in the fridge for up to 3 days.

sweet and spicy strawberry-rhubarb tomato ketchup

YIELD: **about 2 cups**

2 cups chopped rhubarb

1 cup hulled and sliced strawberries

1 tablespoon extra-virgin olive oil

1 small yellow onion, diced

1 garlic clove, minced

3 tablespoons tomato paste

1 (15.5-ounce) can whole peeled tomatoes

¼ cup packed light brown sugar

¼ cup apple cider vinegar

1 teaspoon kosher salt

½ teaspoon whole black peppercorns

½ teaspoon mustard seeds

1 bay leaf

1 cinnamon stick

¼ teaspoon whole allspice

½ teaspoon whole cloves

When I was a kid—as with most kids, I would imagine—I was obsessed with ketchup. Anything I could put ketchup on, you better believe it would find its way into, on top of, or around. I'd walk through the house eating ketchup from those little fast-food packets all day long. I've since grown past that stage in life, thankfully, but I still have a sweet spot for ketchup on my eggs and fries. This recipe is for the kid in us all, but with a sophisticated twist because we're adults now.

1. Combine the rhubarb, strawberries, and ½ cup of water in a large pot over medium-high heat. Cook until the rhubarb and strawberries have broken down a bit, and most of the water has been absorbed, 10 to 15 minutes. Remove from the heat and set aside.

2. Place the olive oil in a separate saucepan over medium-high heat. Add the onion and garlic and cook until just beginning to caramelize, about 5 minutes. Stir in the tomato paste and cook for a minute longer.

3. Transfer to a blender or food processor, along with the strawberry-rhubarb mixture and tomatoes (including juices). Purée until smooth. Return to the saucepan, and add the brown sugar, vinegar, and salt.

continued on page 172

sweet and spicy strawberry-rhubarb tomato ketchup
continued

4. Combine the peppercorns, mustard seeds, bay leaf, cinnamon stick, allspice, and cloves in a piece of cheesecloth. Tie into a small bundle, using kitchen twine. Submerge the spice bundle in the rhubarb mixture in the pan and bring to a boil over medium-high heat. Decrease the heat to low and simmer until reduced, thickened, and darker in color, about 2 hours. Make sure to stir occasionally. Discard the spice bundle and allow the ketchup to cool down.

5. Transfer to an airtight container or a jar with a tight-fitting lid and place in the refrigerator until ready to use. Can be kept in the fridge for several weeks.

thai peanut sauce

YIELD: **about 1 cup**

¾ cup creamy peanut butter

¼ cup coconut milk

1½ tablespoons fresh lime juice

1½ tablespoons soy sauce

2 teaspoons Asian fish sauce

2 teaspoons hot sauce

2 teaspoons rice wine vinegar

2 teaspoons grated fresh gingerroot

1 teaspoon dried crushed red pepper

1 garlic clove, minced

2 tablespoons chopped fresh cilantro

Creamy peanut butter gives this sauce a great consistency and also a nutty taste that balances perfectly with the fresh ginger and crushed red pepper. The sweet and spicy flavors work well in our Shrimp Spring Roll Sliders (page 86) and Spicy Thai Tofu Sliders (page 126).

1. Whisk all of the ingredients together with 1½ tablespoons water in a medium bowl until evenly combined. Transfer to an airtight container or jar with a tight-fitting lid and chill for at least 1 hour before using. Can be stored in the fridge for up to 3 days.

acknowledgments

First and foremost, thank you to my family for all of your love and support. You're the reason why I do what I do, and why I continue to do it. This book is a testament to your love. It's all the times I couldn't see you because I was so busy working on it. It's the trips to the movies or the dinners that I missed (but I was there in spirit). This is for you.

The biggest thank-you to my soul mate, Julian Clark, for your unconditional love and support. Thank you for the invaluable inspiration and input while I was writing this book. Whenever I seemed to hit a roadblock, you were always there to help me get over it. You made sure I didn't go crazy. Also, thanks for enduring night after night of cold sliders for dinner without ever complaining. I love you more than you'll ever know.

To Napoleon the Cat Emperor (#napoleonthecatemperor). Thank you for being my unofficial taste tester, whether I liked it or not. You'll never read this because you're a cat, duh. But thanks for being the best first pet, the one my inner child always wanted. You're the coolest cat ever. Meow meow meow. A.k.a., I love you.

To my agent extraordinaire, Judy Linden (and the whole Stonesong team). You're my fairy godmother. My genie with an endless supply of wishes. You're a dream fulfiller. Your kindness and enthusiasm never cease to amaze me. Thanks for dealing with my million and one questions and long-winded e-mails out of the blue. This literally wouldn't have been possible without you. You believed in me and this book from the very beginning and never gave up hope, even when I had.

Thank you to my editor, Jean Lucas, for taking a chance on a dreamer with a blog and an idea that no one else saw as clearly. Our love of sliders has been transformed into a book I'm very proud of. I hope you are, too. Thank you for all of your hard work. You're a hero.

Big thanks to my publisher and all the kind folks at Andrews McMeel Publishing. Y'all have made me a published author, something I never would have dreamed possible. Thanks to everyone who worked so hard on this book, especially the incredibly talented Diane Marsh, who made it a beautiful piece of art.

A million and one thanks to Tam Putnam, for going through this book with a fine-toothed comb and polishing it into a legit and professional-sounding book. You had to deal with all of my awkward jokes, and that's not easy. You put the cherry on top of this sundae.

To my good friend and fellow cat, Joy Wilson. Thank you for giving me a chance. I knew that stalking you on social media was a good idea. Our love of cats and cocktails brought us together, but it's the good times we've had (and continue to have) that'll keep our friendship going strong. Thank you for teaching me so much. It's an honor to call you a co-visionary and an even greater honor to call you my friend. We're just a couple of hounders in the end. What else can a guy ask for?

Many thanks to Kari Stewart: Your guidance and wisdom calmed me down from my first-book-jitters. You're the cat's pajamas and the nicest person I know. For real.

Thank you to Farah Guy, Kay Yamazaki, Jennifer Melendez, Andrew Sauter, and Nichole Gawalis for being such great friends and recipe testers. Your notes and feedback strengthened this book.

Last and certainly not least, thank you to the readers of *The Candid Appetite*. Your continued support, comments, e-mails, and encouraging words are what keep me going. You've allowed me to come into your lives week after week and have continued to follow along. I wouldn't be here without you. Never forget that. I know I won't. You humble me beyond words.

metric conversions and equivalents

metric conversion formulas

TO CONVERT	MULTIPLY
Ounces to grams	Ounces by 28.35
Pounds to kilograms	Pounds by 0.454
Teaspoons to milliliters	Teaspoons by 4.93
Tablespoons to milliliters	Tablespoons by 14.79
Fluid ounces to milliliters	Fluid ounces by 29.57
Cups to milliliters	Cups by 236.59
Cups to liters	Cups by 0.236
Pints to liters	Pints by 0.473
Quarts to liters	Quarts by 0.946
Gallons to liters	Gallons by 3.785
Inches to centimeters	Inches by 2.54

common ingredients and their approximate equivalents

1 cup uncooked white rice = 185 grams
1 cup all-purpose flour = 120 grams
1 stick butter (4 ounces • ½ cup
 • 8 tablespoons) = 115 grams
1 cup butter (8 ounces • 2 sticks
 • 16 tablespoons) = 225 grams
1 cup brown sugar, firmly packed = 225 grams
1 cup granulated sugar = 200 grams

oven temperatures

To convert Fahrenheit to Celsius, subtract 32 from Fahrenheit, multiply the result by 5, then divide by 9.

DESCRIPTION	FAHRENHEIT	CELSIUS	BRITISH GAS MARK
Very cool	200°	95°	0
Very cool	225°	110°	¼
Very cool	250°	120°	½
Cool	275°	135°	1
Cool	300°	150°	2
Warm	325°	165°	3
Moderate	350°	175°	4
Moderately hot	375°	190°	5
Fairly hot	400°	200°	6
Hot	425°	220°	7
Very hot	450°	230°	8
Very hot	475°	245°	9

approximate metric equivalents

VOLUME	
¼ teaspoon	1 milliliter
½ teaspoon	2.5 milliliters
¾ teaspoon	4 milliliters
1 teaspoon	5 milliliters
1¼ teaspoons	6 milliliters
1½ teaspoons	7.5 milliliters
1¾ teaspoons	8.5 milliliters
2 teaspoons	10 milliliters
1 tablespoon (½ fluid ounce)	15 milliliters
2 tablespoons (1 fluid ounce)	30 milliliters
¼ cup	60 milliliters
⅓ cup	80 milliliters
½ cup (4 fluid ounces)	120 milliliters
⅔ cup	160 milliliters
¾ cup	180 milliliters
1 cup (8 fluid ounces)	240 milliliters
1¼ cups	300 milliliters
1½ cups (12 fluid ounces)	360 milliliters
1⅔ cups	400 milliliters
2 cups (1 pint)	460 milliliters
3 cups	700 milliliters
4 cups (1 quart)	0.95 liter
1 quart plus ¼ cup	1 liter
4 quarts (1 gallon)	3.8 liters

WEIGHT	
¼ ounce	7 grams
½ ounce	14 grams
¾ ounce	21 grams
1 ounce	28 grams
1¼ ounces	35 grams
1½ ounces	42.5 grams
1⅔ ounces	45 grams
2 ounces	57 grams
3 ounces	85 grams
4 ounces (¼ pound)	113 grams
5 ounces	142 grams
6 ounces	170 grams
7 ounces	198 grams
8 ounces (½ pound)	227 grams
16 ounces (1 pound)	454 grams
35.25 ounces (2.2 pounds)	1 kilogram

LENGTH	
⅛ inch	3 millimeters
¼ inch	6 millimeters
½ inch	1¼ centimeters
1 inch	2½ centimeters
2 inches	5 centimeters
2½ inches	6 centimeters
4 inches	10 centimeters
5 inches	13 centimeters
6 inches	15¼ centimeters
12 inches (1 foot)	30 centimeters

Information compiled from a variety of sources, including *Recipes into Type* by Joan Whitman and Dolores Simon (Newton, MA: Biscuit Books, 1993); *The New Food Lover's Companion* by Sharon Tyler Herbst (Hauppauge, NY: Barron's, 2013); and *Rosemary Brown's Big Kitchen Instruction Book* (Kansas City, MO: Andrews McMeel, 1998).

index

Andrews McMeel Publishing
a division of Andrews McMeel Universal
1130 Walnut Street, Kansas City, Missouri 64106

www.andrewsmcmeel.com

16 17 18 19 20 SDB 10 9 8 7 6 5 4 3 2 1

ISBN: 978-1-4494-7604-5

Library of Congress Control Number: 2015954531

Editor: Jean Z. Lucas
Art Director: Diane Marsh
Creative Director: Tim Lynch
Production Editor: Maureen Sullivan
Production Manager: Carol Coe
Demand Planner: Sue Eikos

"After flipping through this book, all I can say is . . .
SLIDERS? YES, PLEASE!!!"
—Paul Lowe, founder of *Sweet Paul* magazine